Spelling S..... .
The Essential How to Spell Guide

Second Edition

Joanne Rudling
www.howtospell.co.uk

"I have made this book recommended reading for my level three law students. Many of these students have struggled with A levels and need a lot of support. I also have mature students who are starting their second career. I think your site, book, and tips are very effective." L.P Martin, Senior Lecturer Law, Staffordshire University, UK

"I am the type of learner that needs to understand why something is the way it is. Kids also like to know why and not just memorize words. I'm not intimidated by spelling and can answer awkward questions about it now. I really only got that from your program and books I appreciate you so MUCH!" Maria Parada, 4th grade teacher, USA

"Great book. I have only just noticed that **ease** is in pl**ease**. Spelling is becoming clearer. For me, it's about putting words together and remembering patterns. It's amazing that if I don't use a few words for 6 to 8 weeks I forget how to spell them." Darren Johnson, construction company director, UK

Spelling Strategies & Secrets:
The Essential How to Spell Guide
by Joanne Rudling

Second edition

© 2019 Joanne Rudling

ISBN: 9781096168492

Published by
How to Spell Publishing

All photos paid for and royalty free from depositphotos.com
or free from openclipart.org and pixabay.com

Thanks to pixabay.com/users/Ben Kerckx (See *ecstatic*)

Contents

Introduction

The purpose of *Spelling Strategies & Secrets* is to help you improve and remember spellings, as well as to increase your spelling knowledge so that you understand why it is the "weird" way it is.

You're going to learn all about spelling strategies and memory tricks to help you recall tricky spellings for words like *necessary, believe, separate, embarrassed, independent, occurred,* and *accommodation.* These are some of the most commonly misspelled words, and some of the most useful words to know how to spell. We might not need these words all the time, but when we do, we want to be able to spell them quickly, correctly, and without panicking and going for another word that we can spell but doesn't express exactly how we feel.

→ You're going to learn various strategies, such as:
- using memory tricks (mnemonics);
- seeing words-within-words;
- noticing vowels;
- learning the history of words and silent letters;
- using syllable breakdown;
- understanding how words are built with prefixes and suffixes;
- sounding words out and rhyming words;
- identifying word families and letter patterns;
- learning some spelling rules.

Using different spelling strategies to help you remember spellings is the aim. You might even use a couple of these strategies on one word.

You'll see concepts and words repeated so it reinforces learning, because it might take a few goes at getting these strategies and memory tricks into your brain.

→ We'll also look at some myths about spelling to really understand what it takes to spell well, and why it's difficult.

→ We'll look at some systems of spelling that can help you learn and teach spelling. Spelling needs to be learnt* as a separate subject because it's a complex thing (*see Style Notes about *learnt* vs. *learned*).

If you don't want to write in this book, then grab a notebook and write, draw, scribble your thoughts, feelings, memory tricks, and the words you want to learn.

The aim of this book is to give you all the information you need about spelling so that you won't get so frustrated with it anymore, and to give you the confidence to spell well.

I want you to know that you can use these strategies to help you spell tricky words, and know that it's not "cheating." We have so many spelling variations and such a huge vocabulary that we need little reminders to spell some words. Even great spellers use them.

This book is not about learning obscure words but about learning common, everyday words that are some of the most misspelled in British English (BrE) and American English (AmE).

It's important that you learn the words that you need for your life, work, education, and leisure. Use a notebook to log these, especially the words you have problems with, and think about how you can use the strategies in this book to help you remember how to spell them.

It's never too late to learn spelling. All it takes is motivation and a need to be able to spell well, whether it's for your job, a course, writing reports, or helping your kids with their homework.

To learn spelling, you need to study it, learn the rules and exceptions, notice the common letter patterns (also called letter strings), know how words are built with prefixes and suffixes, and write — using the spellings.

Using a combination of well-known, proven literacy techniques and spelling strategies, this book will help you learn, remember, and improve your spellings while reinforcing and building

- spelling knowledge
- confidence
- love of spelling and writing

Ready for the journey?

Enjoy spelling, enjoy learning, and enjoy writing.

Style Notes

-ize and *-ise (realise/realize)* are both correct in British English, but American English only uses *-ize*. I use *-ize* throughout this book because *-ize* is the preferred house style of the *Oxford Dictionary*. Some quotes are from British authors and use "ise," such as in *analyse/analysing*, which I'll keep in the quote.

If there are British English (BrE) and American English (AmE) spelling differences, then I write them side by side. It's always good to know the differences because it stops you from getting confused when a red squiggly line appears under a word on your computer screen.

---

learnt/learned,   *spelt/spelled,*   *burnt/burned,*   *spoilt/spoiled,*
misspelt/misspelled, *smelt/smelled,*   *spilt/spilled*   *dwelt/dwelled*

I first learnt all this in 1996. British English (BrE)
I first learned all this in 1996. American English (AmE)

BrE uses both endings, but AmE only uses the –ed ending.

We hardly ever see the –t verb ending in American English, other than *knelt*. *Leapt* is popular, although *leaped* is still the official standard.

There are also some punctuation differences, too, with regards to the Oxford comma (serial comma), and punctuation inside the quotation marks for American English or outside for British English. These don't alter the meaning, so hopefully they won't be too jarring.

I use single quotation marks   — 'like these' — and double for speech/pronunciation/syllables — "like these". Single quotation marks are used more in British English but American English prefer double quotation marks. I prefer the single quotation marks because they aren't so bulky when using them with single letters, for example, 's' vs. "s".

The abbreviation of **versus**.
The common ways to abbreviate *versus* are
British English = **v, vs,** or **vs.** — *Liverpool v Manchester United, good v evil*
American English = **v.** or **vs.** — *Red Sox vs. Yankees, good vs. evil*

Style guides (grammar and punctuation guides), dictionaries, newspapers, and legal documents can vary in the choice of abbreviation, but in formal writing use the full word *versus* — *Wade versus Rowe*.

My Story (see *Your Spelling Stories* at the back)

I've been a lecturer and teacher trainer in literacy, writing, English, and ESOL for 23 years. I use and love all the strategies in this book, and have done so ever since I first learned all about them when I started my literacy teacher training.

Before I became a teacher, I was interested in acting and scriptwriting. While doing a degree in TV and Film Scriptwriting, at age 30, I realized I had problems with my spelling, especially with homophones (they're/their/ there, to/too, it's/its, etc.), and grammar problems (I'd/I'll, etc.). Punctuation was a nightmare, too. Lecturers kept correcting all these problems. For years before this, I'd received rejections for my writing, maybe because of these issues. Even so, I didn't do anything to improve apart from trying to be aware of some of my common mistakes. I had no context to help me remember which homophone was which or where to put apostrophes.

Then one day in 1996, I was walking past Bournemouth Adult Education Centre and something inside told me to go in and offer to do some voluntary work, helping with reading and writing. Thus my teaching journey began. During an induction session, I heard about spelling strategies for adults and I was so excited, but also gobsmacked that I was never taught these.

Now, 20+ years later, I have my own website, www.howtospell.co.uk, which helps thousands of adults throughout the world gain confidence in their spelling, and this includes both British and American English users. I've written online courses available on udemy.com, and many books, including *Spelling Rules Workbook, Punctuation Guide & Workbook, How to Spell the 20 Most Misspelled Words, Why English Spelling is so Weird and Wonderful, Spelling Rules and Patterns for Ages 10-11,* and *Spelling Patterns and Rules for 5th Graders.*

If I can improve my spelling, you can too. All it takes is a big dose of determination, a bit of hard work, a keen eye to notice the rules and patterns of English, and lots of practise writing and using the spellings that are important in your life and work.

The Most Common Misspelled Words

Below are the most commonly misspelled words according to the *Oxford English Dictionary Online* and *Oxford English Corpus*.

According to the Oxford Dictionary, not everyone spells these words incorrectly — *but lots of people do! From sneaky silent letters to devious double letters, English sure doesn't make spelling easy.*
Thanks to blog.oxforddictionaries.com

Can you spell these words? Do you use any strategies to help you?
What are the words and bits you find tricky?

accommodation — 47

accessory — 44, 124, 153

achieve — 33, 55, 87, 147, 152, 202

apparent/ly — 33, 49, 91

appearance/disappearance — 49, 93, 127

argument — 33, 95, 152

basically — 151

beginning — 154, 159, 203

because — 41, 43, 50, 108

believe — 31, 53, 55, 136, 152, 165, 169

beautiful — 108, 114, 144, 146, 1501, 153

business — 34, 64, 153, 155, 184

calendar — 34, 53

Caribbean — 46

cemetery — 53, 54, 123

changeable — 152, 159

colleague — 203

coming — 152

committee — 48, 154, 203

completely — 48, 151

conscious — 143

conscience — 34, 55

definite/definitely — 34, 53, 54, 151, 178

desert/dessert — 69, 75

dilemma — 29-32, 48

disappear — 49, 127

disappoint — 49, 95, 165

disapprove/disapproval — 49

discipline — 54

ecstasy — 121

ecstatic — 35, 151

embarrass — 43, 45, 95, 147

environment — 36, 41, 95, 202

equipment — 95, 147, 154

existence — 54

exhilarate — 32, 118, 144

familiar — 35, 203

finally — 151, 159

fluorescent — 37, 94

foreign — 55, 65, 142

forty — 43

un/foreseeable — 152

forward — 204

friend — 12, 35, 41, 55, 162-165

government — 36, 95, 147

grateful — 146, 178

guarantee — 62, 152

harass — 45, 95, 147

A quickie quiz

This is to get your brain going. Don't worry if you make mistakes or don't know which is correct — that's absolutely fine. We're going to look at lots of ways to remember these spellings throughout the book.

Which is correct?

1. a. tomorrow
   b. tommorow

2. a. accomadation
   b. accommodation

3. a. necessary
   b. neccessary

4. a. enviroment
   b. environment

5. a. truly
   b. truely

6. a. seperate
   b. separate

Check your choices in the list above or on the previous page.

The Secrets of Spelling

Myth-busting: Secrets of spelling that shouldn't be secret!

Let's start off by looking at some important facts and bust some common myths about spelling.

Negative attitudes about spelling can create barriers to learning, which means they can stop you from learning how to spell well, stop you from expressing yourself in writing, and can even stop you writing altogether.

Understanding spelling and why it works the way that it does will help prevent you from getting frustrated with it, so you start loving and improving it.

Questions to get you thinking about spelling:

1. Does reading improve spelling?

2. Is English spelling totally irregular?

3. What percentage of words have silent letters in them?

4. Why do we have silent letters?

5. Why don't we spell the way we speak?

1. Reading vs. Spelling

Reading is very important, but it *won't* improve your spelling. It requires different skills. Spelling is much more difficult than reading, so don't beat yourself up because you're a good reader but a bad speller. People from all walks of life, including professional academics, can have spelling problems.

> → Look at and say the following words. They have the same long vowel sound, 'e' + 's', but with 7 different spellings.
>
> **knees**, **please**, **freeze**, **Chinese**, **fleas**, **seize**, **cheese**
>
> Easy to read, but not so easy to spell!

So reading doesn't really help spelling, but knowing all about spelling — how words are built with prefixes and suffixes, understanding rules, exceptions and their patterns, and identifying common letter patterns — can help your reading.

You won't learn how to spell just by reading, because improving spelling means you have to consciously notice patterns and rules, and you don't do that when you read! A word must be consciously and deliberately learnt.

We skim over words when we read, whereas when we spell, we are engaged in an active, letter-by-letter activity.

> Teachers assume that reading, once taught, automatically means that spelling will be "caught." But there is no correlation between reading ability and spelling ability. Spelling uses a set of active, productive, conscious processes that are not required for reading.
>
> David Crystal: *The English Language*

> According to Templeton & Bear, reading ability in children is ahead of their spelling ability. Many of them can read words like *shopping* and *bottle,* but spell them *shoping* and *botel.* This is true for adults too.
>
> → Do you know why *shopping* is spelled with a double 'p', and *bottle* with a double 't'? You'll discover why in the Spelling Rules, and Phonic Spelling Strategies sections.

2. Is English spelling chaotic and totally irregular?

English spelling isn't chaotic, just complicated, with historical reasons for why it is the way it is. If you know these reasons, then you'll start to understand and respect spelling a lot more, and maybe even come to love it. We'll look at some of these reasons throughout the book.

English spelling is much more regular than we think. In fact, 75% of the time, it's regular. But it's true that there are many irregular spellings; this is because English includes words borrowed from many languages, very old words, and silent letters.

"There seems to be both regularity and irregularity in English spelling. English spelling gives the impression of being more irregular than it really is. There are about 400 words in English whose spelling is wholly irregular — the trouble is, these are among the most frequently used words in the language."

Although among answer are aunt autumn blood build
castle climb comb come cough could course
debt do does done dough eye friend gone great
have hour island journey key lamb listen move none
of once one only own people pretty quay receive rough
said salt says shoe shoulder some sugar
talk two was water were where who you

David Crystal: *The English Language*

Notice a lot of these words have silent letters in them. Most silent letters used to be pronounced, and therefore written, but are now silent because of changes in spoken English but not written.

Many silent letters show the history of the word and how it used to be pronounced centuries ago! They're the fossilized remains of a once-spoken letter —little dinosaurs. But we love them for telling us the history of the word!

The English spelling system developed over the centuries, and these irregularities came about because writers, and printers, of varying native languages tried to fit their alphabets and sounds to English. Latin writers, French scribes, the printers in the late 1400s, and the 16th century academics all brought their own "strange" ways of spelling English words based on their native languages. We'll discover how these influenced spelling in the Silent Letters chapter.

Also, there was a dramatic change in pronunciation during the Great Vowel Shift between 1450 and 1750, when many vowel and consonant sounds changed or disappeared. Unfortunately, this happened as spelling became fixed.

Pronunciation is always changing, but we don't alter spellings or we'd be forever changing them. And anyway, which pronunciation would we use as a benchmark for spelling? My Midlands accent, London accents, American, Australian?

3. 60% of English words have silent letters in them

Silent letters can cause all sorts of problems with spelling a word or looking it up in a dictionary. But if you know the history of why there are silent letters, it'll not only improve your spelling, but also prevent frustration with it (for more information, please see the Silent Letter chapter).

4. Why do we have silent letters?

Centuries ago spelling was phonetic — people used to spell how they spoke. Most of today's silent letters used to be pronounced, so they were reflected in their spellings. Pronunciation is forever changing, but the spelling system doesn't reflect this. For example, *knock, knee, knuckle, gnaw, gnat* are all Viking/Old Norse words. The 'k' and 'g' used to be pronounced, then slowly dropped out of fashion.

Sometimes, the way something is spelled shows us the history of the word and the way people spoke it centuries ago — and that's why the spelling might seem a bit strange.

(We'll see more about why we have silent letters in the Silent Letters Chapter)

5. Why don't we spell the way we speak?

To have a standardized, phonetic "sounding out" system that works, there would have to be only one way of spelling each sound. This is true in some languages, but not English.

There have always been many different accents in English and to decide which accent, or dialect, to base the spelling on would be impossible, and always has been impossible.

English has never had an academy of English to oversee grammar, vocabulary, and spelling. For centuries, people spelt how they wanted to. It was only in 1830 that a group of academics decided to write the definitive dictionary of English spelling (later to become the *Oxford Dictionary*). These men weren't interested in making spelling simple, or linking it to pronunciation, or making English easy to read. Pacquita Boston in her book, *The Inside Story of Spelling*, says that their task was to choose a spelling "they felt best reflected the history or origin of each word. They often had a great range of spellings to choose from. They unified spelling, but did not simplify it." (See chapter on Silent Letters.)

Phonics is one of five systems/ways that can help us learn to spell. Good spellers often try to sound out an unfamiliar spelling to see if it sounds like a pattern they know. They then write it down to see if it looks right. Often, the spelling does reflect pronunciation and can give clues, or very clear indications, of likely spelling: *light, right, bright; thick, sick, lick, trick* (see the chapters on Spelling Systems, Letter Patterns, and Phonics).

Handwriting

Always write and type in lower case (small letters) with capitals for proper nouns. It's easier to write in and means you can see the shape of the word:

education Britain *brilliant* **words**

Writing or typing a lot trains your muscle memory to remember the shape, feel, and flow of the word, and soon it'll seem like the words are spelling themselves.

Block capitals are ALL CAPITALS. Never write in block capitals unless it's on a form because it's hard to write in and hard to see the shape of the words you are spelling.

As well as having a visual memory and an auditory memory, we also have a motor memory. This is to do with movement. Our muscles can 'remember' shape and movement so that when we write a word, they will form an imprint of the flow and pattern of the letters, especially if using cursive, "joined up" writing.

Anne Betteridge: *Adult Learners' Guide to Spelling.*

Dictionaries

Knowing the meaning of words, as well as knowing how to use them, is an important strategy in learning a word or spelling.

Don't be afraid of looking in a dictionary to check not only the spelling, but also the meaning of a word and how it is used in context in a sentence. With some online dictionaries, you can check the pronunciation, too.

Put these on your favourites/favorites bar or bookmark them so you can access them all the time.

www.oxforddictionaries.com - British & American
www.macmillandictionary.com - British & American
http://dictionary.cambridge.org - British & American
www.merriam-webster.com - American online

According to David Crystal, using dictionaries is important because spelling does not stand still. It changes with the times, as do features of language, such as vocabulary and grammar. A surprising number of words in a general dictionary vary in the way they can be written: is it moon or Moon, flowerpot or flower-pot, judgment or judgement?

The Do's and Don'ts of Spelling

(**do's** can also be spelt/spelled **dos**)

Do learn about spelling — it's never too late to learn to spell. If you really want to spell well, then learn the rules and exceptions, notice letter patterns, learn how words are built with prefixes and suffixes, and understand why we spell the way we do.

Do write as often as you can. Also, write in lowercase/small letters, with capitals in the right places for proper nouns, such as Joanne, Britain, and Canada. This means you can see the shape of the word. Also, use the capital I — I, I'm, I've, I'll, I'd.

Don't write in BLOCK CAPITALS unless it's on a form because it's hard to write in and to read.

Do use the words you like even if you're not sure of the spelling. If you need help, ask someone, or try to use a dictionary or spellchecker.

Do try to find your own errors. Proofread your emails, comments, and messages, and go over them again and again. Go over your writing slowly and read it out loud to see if you've missed any words, missed letters, or wrote the wrong word, especially homophones. Be careful with predictive text; it's convenient, but it might give you a weird, totally incorrect word.

Do make a correct copy of the words you need to learn for your life, work, training, and education —make a little dictionary for yourself and use the Look Say Cover Write Check method (see the chapter on this for more details).

Do write the words you want to use, and test yourself regularly.

Don't look at or concentrate on the wrong spelling (remember, your visual memory is strong). Figure out what your mistakes are, and then concentrate on the correct spelling and how to remember it.

Don't learn words you'll never use. Concentrate on those you need.

Don't try to learn too many words at once. Pick the most important keywords for your work, life, and education.

Don't rely on the sound of the word for its spelling. Think about it in as many ways as you can —its look, meaning, sound, feel...

Do use memory tricks and spelling strategies.

Do enjoy spelling for all its quirkiness, and stay passionate about your learning and life.

Glossary of Terms

> ➔ Do you know these key terms that can help you understand spelling?
> nouns, proper nouns, singular and plural nouns, adjectives, homophones
> verbs, third person verbs
> prefixes, suffixes, and root words
> syllables and syllable breakdown

Nouns are things, places, or people: *table, chair, London, Joanne...*
Singular nouns = *a dog, a watch, a chair, a bus pass...*
Plural nouns = *dogs, watches, chairs, bus passes...*
Proper nouns start with a capital letter = *Joanne, London, America...*

A memory trick to remember what a noun is 'n' in noun = name

Adjectives describe nouns: a *blue* bag, a *happy* baby, a *boring* life...
Some adjectives have -**ing** and -**ed** suffix endings:
She's *excited*. This is *interesting*. It's not *boring*...

Homophones are words that have the same sound but different spelling and meaning: *there/they're/their, to/too/two, your/you're, stationary/stationery...*

Verbs show action or being: you *work*, I *watched*, they *are*, we *listen*, I *read*, you're *learning* and *reading* this...
Third-person means using *he, she, or it* for a subject and we add 's' or 'es' to root verbs: *he sees, she runs, it moves, he watches, she wishes...*

Prefixes and Suffixes

prefix + **root word** + suffix
uncomfortable

Prefixes are little words we put on **root words** to change their meaning and grammar — **mis**understand**ing**, **im**maturely
prefixes = in-, un-, mis-, dis-, im-, il-, sub-, pre-...
suffixes = -ed, -ing, -tion, -able, -ible, -er, -or...
(More information in the Building Words with Prefixes & Suffixes chapter.)

Syllable breakdown is about breaking a word down into little spoken chunks, where each chunk usually has a vowel in it:
1 syllable: trick
2 syllables: paper — "pa-per"
3 syllables: computer — "com-pu-ter"
4 syllables: application — "ap-pli-ca-tion"
5 syllables: uncomfortable — "un-com-for-ta-ble" or "un-com-fort-able"
(More details in the Syllable Breakdown chapter.)

Spelling Systems

In this section, we're looking at some interesting ways of learning spelling from some experts. Use or try whatever interests you.

A System for Spelling (thanks to the Basic Skills Agency)

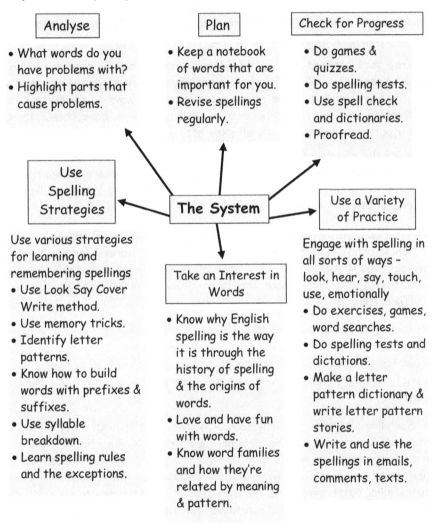

Analyse
- What words do you have problems with?
- Highlight parts that cause problems.

Plan
- Keep a notebook of words that are important for you.
- Revise spellings regularly.

Check for Progress
- Do games & quizzes.
- Do spelling tests.
- Use spell check and dictionaries.
- Proofread.

Use Spelling Strategies
Use various strategies for learning and remembering spellings
- Use Look Say Cover Write method.
- Use memory tricks.
- Identify letter patterns.
- Know how to build words with prefixes & suffixes.
- Use syllable breakdown.
- Learn spelling rules and the exceptions.

The System

Use a Variety of Practice
Engage with spelling in all sorts of ways – look, hear, say, touch, use, emotionally
- Do exercises, games, word searches.
- Do spelling tests and dictations.
- Make a letter pattern dictionary & write letter pattern stories.
- Write and use the spellings in emails, comments, texts.

Take an Interest in Words
- Know why English spelling is the way it is through the history of spelling & the origins of words.
- Love and have fun with words.
- Know word families and how they're related by meaning & pattern.

Five Spelling Systems

Good spellers use all sorts of methods to learn and remember spellings. In this section, we'll look at some of these in more detail, but don't worry about the technical terms; just know that these are suggestions about how we learn, or can learn, to spell, and how we can combine many of these "systems" to help us.

According to academic, teacher, and author, Johanna Stirling, there are five useful systems/ways of learning spelling:

1. Know the history of spelling (the *Etymological System*). This method is about knowing the history of English spelling and why we spell words the way that we do. Stirling says this is one of the most important ways to really learn and understand English spelling because it explains why we have those strange letter patterns like -ough, -igh, wh-, kn-, etc.

Knowing the history of English spelling will also help you feel less frustrated and annoyed with spelling. We'll look at why difficult words are spelled the way they are in the chapters on Silent Letters, Letter Patterns, Word Families, and Taking an Interest in Words.

2. Know how words are built (the *Morphological System*). Think about words morphing/changing when adding small words to a root word! By adding prefixes and suffixes to root words, you change the meaning - *uncomfortable, unhappy, dissatisfied*, etc. More about this in the Building Words with Prefixes and Suffixes chapter.

3. Seeing patterns and links (the *Lexical System*). This is a very interesting system. It focuses on word families with the same letter patterns and related meanings (not the phonetic/sound link): *two, twice, twelve, between... sign, signal, signify, signpost...* We'll see more about this in the Word Families chapter.

4. Sounding out words (the *Phonological System*). This is about using the sounds of words to help us spell. English is only about 45-50% phonetically regular, so it's tricky relying on phonics. But we tend to try to sound out words when we don't know how to spell a new/strange word, and we do this to hear if it relates to a spelling pattern we know. We then use our visual memory to see if it looks right. We'll see some useful strategies for the Phonological System in the Phonetic Strategies chapter.

5. Seeing spelling patterns and rules (the *Graphemic System*). This method concentrates on seeing letter patterns, understanding word endings and learning some spelling rules. We'll discuss this further in the sections on Visual Spelling Patterns, Suffixes, and Spelling Rules.

More interesting thoughts from some spelling experts.

As your knowledge of words increases, your confidence in learning improves, your ability to use a dictionary develops and your memory bank of words grow larger, you will start being able to predict likely spelling patterns or feel able to learn whole groups of words at once, and learning and remembering spellings will become easier for YOU.

Basic Skills Agency's *The Spelling Pack*

Analysing (Analyzing — AmE) your own errors can help you greatly in gaining confidence in yourself as learners, and in developing appropriate and effective strategies for learning spelling.

Klein: *Learning to Spell — or Spelling to Learn*

There are five ways into a word:
1. Think about the meaning of the word.
2. Unpack the way the word is making that meaning by looking for the base word (root word), prefixes and suffixes.
3. Find out where the word has come from.
4. Listen to the sounds in the word.
5. Check if any spelling rules apply.

Good spellers use all of these strategies. Poor spellers rely on sounds!

English spelling is not an illogical burden there to make life difficult for our children. If we are not simultaneously teaching students [and adults] the phonology, orthography, morphology and etymology of words, then we are not giving them all the pieces of the spelling puzzle – and their struggles will be our failure.

Misty Adoniou
Senior Lecturer in Language, Literacy at University of Canberra

https://theconversation.com/does-your-child-struggle-with-spelling-this-might-help-104410

English spelling must engage the eyes as well as an understanding of word meaning and spelling structure to help the brain register where and why letters appear in the patterns that they do.

Sally Raymond: *Spelling Rules, Riddles and Remedies*

Knowing the story behind why a word is spelled in a certain way helps kids [and adults] see that spelling isn't the illogical mess they think it is.

David Crystal

Increasingly, however, pupils also need to understand the role of **morphology** and **etymology**. National Curriculum for schools UK

Can you remember these from the Five Spelling Systems?

Notes	Thoughts and questions

Dyslexia Help

Dyslexic spelling help from **beatingdyslexia.com**

According to the lovely people at beatingdyslexia.com: "... remembering how words are spelt in more than one way will give you a stronger and more precise memory of them. This is called creating layers of memory."

Remembering with your eyes:
This is about using the visual appearance of words to remember how they are spelt: *tendency*

Remembering with your ears:
Pronouncing a word the way it is written is a classic spelling tip. Say it out loud, the way it is spelt, to make it stick in your mind: *iron "I ron"*

Remembering with your brain:
This one is about how the English language works. Every rule in English was made to be broken. It's a better idea to look at the letter patterns:
joke — joking (drop the 'e' with –ing rule)

Remembering with your imagination:
This is about using imagination and association to remember how words are spelt: *possession* — the s's are guarding the 'e'

www.beatingdyslexia.com/spelling-tips

➔ We'll see more from beatingdyslexia.com in the Spotting Vowels section.

www.beatingdyslexia.com/vowel-lessons

Focus on only the vowels: *When I'm learning to spell a new word the first thing I do is focus on only the vowels. I remember misspelling the word sentence. If we look at only the vowels in the word 'sentence', we can see they are all e's.*

sentence

Spelling pep talk — making mistakes is good

As adults, we feel so stupid when we make mistakes. We give ourselves a hard time about it, and even hate ourselves for it. And making spelling mistakes, or not knowing how something is spelt, is right up there.

> According to a report by the NRDC on adult writing, spelling was identified as the "bit of writing" that's the most difficult.
> **Q2. Which bits of writing are difficult?**
> 52 per cent said spelling was the most difficult
> 9.9 per cent said punctuation
> 9.9 per cent said grammar   Kelly, Soundranayagam, Grief

Spelling can be learned — it just takes a bit of time, effort, and thinking about to fix mistakes we have internalized.

Don't get stressed if you forget a spelling. Just because you learn something or see a word spelt once, it doesn't mean you'll remember it. You have to keep working on the spelling to commit it to your long-term memory. You'll probably have to keep working on the memory tricks you come up with, too.

Remember, you need to keep practising/practicing (AmE) spelling and keep writing, which I'm sure you do with social media comments and emails. So don't give yourself a hard time; instead, know that you're doing a little bit every day to improve your spelling.

> Just because you have seen a word and copied it down once, does not mean it's yours. You won't "own" that word to use it when you want to without really **learning** it, **committing** it to memory in the first place.
> Basic Skills Agency: Spelling Pack

Studying a word/spelling in a deliberate, active, and conscious way means you need to notice the features of words. Pay attention to how words are made up of letter patterns, root words, prefixes, suffixes, and rules. Also, writing and spelling are linked, so write.

If you divide your notes like this, it improves your memory retention:

Notes	Thoughts and questions

Remember that you forget the most information in the first few hours after you learn it so you need to:

- revise/review little but often;
- revise/review a newly learned word/memory trick within 20 seconds or so, and then review it again an hour later;
- get a good night's sleep, which helps memorization; try looking at a new word before bed, and then again in the morning;
- not leave it more than a week before you revise/review a new word;
- use the word in your writing, or take a real, conscious note of it when you see the word in print, online, or in ads.

What good spellers have in common is they:
- use different strategies to remember spellings
- can see patterns and regularity in spelling
- are interested in words, their origins, meaning, and spelling
- can see errors when proofreading
- can break words into syllables/parts and spell those parts
- can hear new words and link them to letter patterns
- recognize letter patterns
- know spelling rules and exceptions
- have a strong visual memory can see a word in their mind, or see if a word looks right.

You must work at and study spelling -
notice it, think about it, question it, and take notes.

Taking notes, writing your thoughts, and questioning helps
to boost your retention/remembering by 50%.

And, of course, you must write and use the spellings.

> Enjoy. Have fun. Be inspired.

Self-Assessment Exercise 1

Which is correct?

Warning! Multiple choice exercises can really mess with your brain. Seeing a similar-looking spelling can really throw you, so that's why it's important to be able to use various spelling strategies to help you figure out which is which for this type of exercise. But for now, use this as a self-assessment exercise, and don't worry about getting it right - mistakes are good

1. a. weird   b. wierd

2. a. accommodate   b. accommdate

3. a. truely   b. truly

4. a. cemetary   b. cemetery

5. a. supercede   b. supersede

6. a. ecstacy   b. ecstasy

7. a. Caribbean   b. Carribean

8. a. harass   b. harrass

9. a. embarass   b. embarrass

10. a. maintainence   b. maintenance

11. a. pronunciation   b. pronounciation

12. a. definately   b. definitely

13. a. business   b. buisness

Answers

Did you use any strategies? Did you see what looked right?
Did seeing the other spellings confuse you? We'll look at
these words and how to remember them in the book.

1. a. weird ~~b. wierd~~

2. a. accommodate ~~b. accommodate~~

3. ~~a. truely~~ b. truly

4. ~~a. cemetary~~ b. cemetery

5. ~~a. supercede~~ b. supersede

6. ~~a. ecstacy~~ b. ecstasy

7. a. Caribbean ~~b. Carribean~~

8. a. harass ~~b. harrass~~

9. ~~a. embarras~~ b. embarrass

10. ~~a. maintainence~~ b. maintenance

11. a. pronunciation ~~b. pronounciation~~

12. ~~a. definately~~ b. definitely

13. a. business ~~b. buisness~~

Notes
What words do you need to work on?

Self-Assessment Exercise 2

Which of these words is correct?

Remember, these types of exercises are only useful when you can use your spelling strategies to help remember which is which. Then again, you might be able to use your visual memory to see what's right.

1. a. dilemma   b. dillemma   c. dillema

2. a. necessary   b. neccessary   c. necesary

3. a. miniscule   b. minusscule   c. minuscule

4. a. milennium   b. millennium   c. millenium

5. a. accesory   b. acessory   c. accessory

6. a. separately   b. seperately   c. separatly

7. a. tommorrow   b. tommorow   c. tomorrow

8. a. comittee   b. committee   d. commitee

9. a. supercede   b. supersede   c. superceed

10. a. ocurred   b. occured   c. occurred

11. a. irresistable   b. irresstible   c. irresistible

Answers

1. a. dilemma ~~b. dillemma~~ ~~c. dillema~~

2. a. necessary ~~b. neccessary~~ ~~c. necesary~~

3. ~~a. miniscule~~ ~~b. minusscule~~ c. minuscule

4. ~~a. milennium~~ b. millennium ~~c. millenium~~

5. ~~a. accesory~~ ~~b. acessory~~ c. accessory

6. a. separately ~~b. seperately~~ ~~c. separatly~~

7. ~~a. tommorrow~~ ~~b. tommorow~~ c. tomorrow

8. ~~a. comittee~~ b. committee ~~d. commitee~~

9. ~~a. supercede~~ b. supersede ~~c. superceed~~

10. ~~a. ocurred~~ ~~b. occured~~ c. occurred

11. ~~a. irresisteble~~ ~~b. irresistible~~ c. irresistible

Notes

We're going to look at how to remember these words using various strategies.

27

Spelling Strategies — the Tricks to Remember Spelling

➜ Do you use any "tricks" to help you remember a spelling?

Using spelling strategies/memory aids to remember how to spell difficult words is one of the most important aspects of spelling.

It's reassuring to know you can use a variety of spelling strategies to help you recall spellings, and in this book, we're going to look at strategies such as:

- Using memory tricks (mnemonics).
- Seeing a word within a word.
- Seeing vowels.
- Noticing prefixes and suffixes.
- Seeing letter patterns.
- Recognising word families linked by meaning.
- Using syllable breakdown.
- Using rhymes, phrases, and acronyms.
- Understanding the history of spelling and why some words are spelled the way they are.
- Knowing spelling rules.

You might find that some of these spelling strategies are very useful and work for you, and some you won't like or find useful — that's OK and normal. This is a chance to try, and learn, some of the best strategies to help your spelling.

Other people's memory tricks are useful to know and use, but if you invent your own, the process of coming up with one will help fix it in your brain.

Use whatever works, makes sense, and is logical for you. You might use different strategies for the same word — that's also OK.

When using memory tricks to remember a spelling:
- have fun;
- use humour/humor (AmE);
- be outrageous, rude, bawdy (you'll remember it then!);
- give the word an emotional attachment;
- draw or doodle a picture of the memory trick and word (this engages the brain to make strong memory links).

Mnemonics are memory aids/memory tricks to help you remember spellings. They could be a sentence, special word, phrase, a short poem, or a rhyme. We're going to look at lots of these, but you don't need to remember all of them, only the ones you need. If the memory trick doesn't work for you, make up one that does.

Don't worry about whether you'll forget these strange but very useful mnemonics — deep down in those brain cells, they're there! And something will trigger the recall of *Emma and her dilemma,* or *the permanent resident in the tent,* or the *envelopes in stationery.*

Next, we're going to look at the word-within-word strategy, and use some of the techniques below (and throughout the book).

The storage and recall of spelling is all about hearing, seeing, writing, drawing, deep thinking, emotions. All these activities fire neurons in the brain:

1. Adopting the role of "spelling detective" actively promotes thinking and reasoning skills.

2. Using memory prompts captures interest and thought, but needs to be rehearsed and revised/reviewed (AmE).

3. Drawing pictures engages the brain in developing strong memory traces [in the 'Note' sections, draw and doodle if the mood takes you].

4. Recall spelling through different activities.

Sally Raymond: *Spelling Rules, Riddles and Remedies*

Word-within-words preparation exercise

Which is correct?

1. believe or beleive?

2. piece or peice?

3. there or their? *There is a place over there.* or
Their is a place is over their.

4. here or hear? *Can you hear that?* or *Can you here that?*

5. separate or seperate?

6. dilemma or dillemma? Answers on the next page.

Words Within Words

Seeing words within words can help you remember the difficult bits of complex words, including the tricky letter patterns (-ie- or –ei-), the silent letters, the double consonants, and which homophone is which. This helps break down long words, too.

Finding words-within-words is another strategy that helps memory of long spellings. The most useful is when we can find words with related meaning that help us to spell.

Johanna Stirling: *Teaching Spelling*

Many words have shorter words inside them. The English language is a difficult language when it comes to spelling, but one good thing about it is that it contains patterns of letters which are repeated again and again. This is why we can find so many words inside other words.

Anne Betteridge: *Adult Learners' Guide to Spelling*

If you're a fan of howtospell.co.uk and my books, then you might have seen, or know, some of these mnemonics because I repeat them again and again; doing so is good because it helps get them into your long-term memory (and I love and use them too).

Answers: believe, piece, there, hear, separate, dilemma

➜ Can you see the word within the word in these tricky words?

1. *believe* — when you don't tell the truth — _____

2. *piece* — you can eat this with a meat or fruit filling — _____

3. *there* — place — _____   (*There is a place is over there.*)

4. *hear* — to listen with this — _____ (*Can you hear that?*)

5. *separate* — an animal is in this word — _____

6. *dilemma* — a girl's name — _____

Answers
1. *bel**ie**ve* — lie
2. ***pie**ce* — pie
3. ***there*** — here
4. *h**ear*** — ear
5. *sepa**rat**e* — rat
6. *dil**emma*** — Emma

When you use the word-within-a-word strategy:

1. See the word in the word.

2. Try to link the "hidden" word to a related saying. Coming up with your own unique saying/sentence will help make the spelling, and memory trick, memorable and gives you a clue to the word in the word. Be as crazy as you want.

3. Draw a picture. Find photos. Remember, drawing a picture engages the brain in developing strong memory links. Visualize the picture it creates in your mind's eye.

believe (tricky bit: -ie-)

1. See the word within the word *bel**ie**ve*

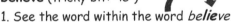

2. Make a sentence — *Never believe a **lie**.*
   *If you **lie**, I won't bel**ie**ve you.*
   *There's a **lie** in believe.*
3. Draw a picture, or imagine it.

piece (*peace* or *piece?*)

1. **Pie** in **pie**ce
2. *I'd like a **piece** of **pie**.*
3. Picture it!

there (*there, their, they're?*)

1. **Here** in t**here**
2. ***Here** t**here** w**here** every**where** no**where**.*
3. Notice the **here** in all the "place" words.

hear (*here* or *hear?*)

1. **Ear** in h**ear**
2. *H**ear** with your **ear** and learn.*   3.
   hear, heard, hearing

separate (tricky bit: -arat-)

1. **rat** in sep**a**rate
2. Separate **a rat**.

   There's **a rat** in sep_a_rate. "sep a rat e"
   Pull a**part** to se**par**ate.
   Never sep**arate** a **para** from his **para**chute.

There's also a rat in exhil_a_rate.

dilemma (tricky bit: double 'm')

1. Emma in dil_emma_
2. **Emma** is in a dil**emma**.
3.

→Which is correct?

1. achievement or acheivement?

2. apparent or aparent?

3. argument or arguement?

4. adress or address?

5. calender or calendar?

6. definitely or definately?

7. diferent or different?

8. enviroment or environment?

Check your answers in the next section.

Key Tricky Words and Their Memory Tricks

Anything goes. Don't shy away from silly or sensational associations. You may even disagree with what your trick sentence says. If it works for you, don't reject it.   Murray Suid: *Demonic Mnemonics*

Thanks to Murray for some of the memory tricks.

Write your tricks in the spaces.
▶

➲ **achieve/achievement** (-ie-)
achieving (drop the 'e' with –ing)

*Eve achieved the achieve*ments she wanted.
*The chief achieved every*thing.
Or use the saying: "i before e except after c."

➲ **apparently**/apparent (2 p's, 2 a's, rent)
apparent + ly = *apparently*   *ap/pa/rent/ly*
*It's apparent that a posh parent can pay the **rent**.*
An app for parents is apparently popular.

➲ **argument** (no 'e')
We usually keep the 'e' when adding -ment, but drop the 'e' in *argument*.
argue + ment = argument

I lost an 'e' in an argument.
I always argue and always lose that e in arguments.
Don't chew gum in an argument.

➲ **address**
add an **address**

➲ **analyse/analyze** (drop the 'e' — *analysing/analyzing*)
analyse is the main British spelling, but *analyze* is acceptable, too.
analyze is the American spelling.
Stop being anal and analysing/analyzing yourself.

➲ **bargain** — *When you get a bargain, you gain.*

➲ **bicycle** — *When it's icy, don't ride your bicycle.*

➲ **business** (tricky bit: *busi*)
We say "biz ness" but the spelling has a **bus** and silent **i**.
*It's good busi**ness** to go by **bus**.*
*Having a busi**ness** is not a **sin**.*

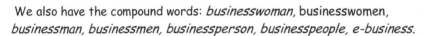

Spelling rule — change the 'y' to 'i' with 'ness'
busy + ness = *business*, happy + ness = *happiness*

We also have the compound words: *businesswoman*, businesswomen,
businessman, businessmen, businessperson, businesspeople, e-business.

➲ **calendar**
*Check your cal**end**ar for **dates** and see if you can **lend a** hand.*
*A calend**ar** is a list of **dates**.*
Len *checks his cale**nd**ar every **day**.*

➲ **conscience** — con + science
*Don't si**lence** your con**science** about **science**.*

➲ **dangerous** (danger + ous) *Anger is **danger**ous.*

➲ **definite/definitely** (tricky bit: the two i's)
definite = de + **finite**   de + **finite** + ly = de**finite**ly
Finite *possibilities are de**finite**.*
Write it definite.
Definite has two i's in it.

In the British TV series *Line of Duty*, a character typed in 'definately' and when
viewers spotted it, they took to Twitter. But this was a clever plot device,
because we saw it being spelled like this again and... (no plot spoilers here).

➲ **different/difference** (tricky bits: double f and –ent)
*I beg to **differ** but the **rent** is **different** every year.*
*What's the **difference** if we **differ** in the **end**?*

➲ **difficult/difficulty** (double f)
difficult + y = difficulty
*The two **f**'s are doubly difficult.*
*See the **cult** in dif**ficult** — **cults** are difficult to fight for.*

➲ **ecstatic**
My _ever_ _crazy_ hair **static** doesn't make me ec**static**.

➲ **ignorant** — _Ignorant people **rant**._

➲ **familiar** — _That **liar** looks famil**iar**._
➲ **peculiar** — _He's a familiar peculiar **liar**._
These words are **peculiar** because they have **unfamiliar** patterns.
They break down into syllables: _"fa-mil-i-ar", "pe-cu-li-ar"_

➲ **friend** — _Is this the **end**, my fri**end**?_
My fri**end** has **fries** at the **end** of the week on **Friday**.
If you **"fri"** your friend, he'll come to an **end**.

➲ **hospital** — _You might have to **spit** in a hospi**tal**._

➲ **instead** — _Drink **tea** inst**ead** of coffee._

➲ **listen** — _Listen to the **list**._

➲ **jealousy** — _Jealousy is **lousy**._

➲ **museum** — _**Use** the mus**eum**._

➲ **neurotic** — _They're **neuro**tic about leaving the **euro** zone._

A quick review exercise:
1. a. aparently   b. apparently
2. a. ignorant   b. ignorent
3. a. musueum   b. museum
4. a. familiar   b. familear
5. a. definitely   b. definately
6. a. calender   b. calendar
7. a. arguement   b. argument
8. a. beleive   b. believe
9. a. acheive   b. achieve   Check your answers on the previous pages.

-ent Letter Pattern

➲ **accident**
When two cars collide, they make a **dent**.
Or: *A Car Crashed made a **dent**.*

➲ **excellent** (tricky bit: double l + ent)
See all the e's: **ex cel lent**. This breaks down into syllables well: "ex-cel-lent".
*Extra **cells** in your brain are ex**cellent**.*

➲ **environment** and **government** (tricky bit: both have a silent 'n')

government = govern + ment

Can you see the **iron** in envi**ron**ment?
*We can **iron** out the envi**ron**ment.*
*A new envi**ron**ment will **iron** it out.*

➲ **independent** (See all those e's — *in de pen dent*)
*The indepen**dent** voters didn't make a **dent** in the election.*
*The inde**pen**dent value of the **pen** depends on the **dent** in it.*

*You can't **dent** the ego of a confi**dent** indepen**dent** pru**dent** stu**dent**.*

➲ **present** — *He **sent** a pre**sent**.*

➲ **permanent** — *The **man** is a perma**nent** resi**dent** of the **tent**.*

➲ **persistent** — *My **sis** is so persis**tent** about getting a **tent**.*
➲ **insistent** — My **sis** was insis**tent** about the **tent**.

➲ **prevalent** — Drinking real **ale** is now preva**lent** everywhere.

➲ **succulent** — *The **cu**cumber he **lent** us was su**cc**u**lent**.*

➲ **measurement** — *Be **sure** to mea**sure** your mea**sure**ments.*

➲ **parliament** — *Liam **went** to the Houses of Parlia**ment**.*
or *I **am** parl**iam**ent.*

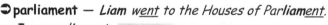

⮱**fluorescent** (begins with fluor-) *flu or e scent*
*I had the **flu** and **spent** the night in a fluorescent **tent**.*
-**escent** pattern: *fluor**escent**, adol**escent**, lumin**escent**,
obsol**escent**, phosphorescent, incandescent, convalescent.*

-**uo**- pattern: fluor**ide**, b**uo**y, b**uo**yant, d**uo**, q**uo**.

A fluorescent buoy.

(➔More –ent words in the Letter Pattern section.)

⮱**secretary** — *A secre**t**ary will keep **a secret**.*

⮱**significant** — Sign if I cant. *"sign if I can't"*
Notice all those i's: sig nif i cant.
This breaks down into syllables well: "sig-nif-i-cant".

⮱**sincerely** — since + rely
 *Since I **rely** on you, I **since**<u>rely</u> need you.*

⮱**soldier** — *Sol**die**rs sometimes **die** in battle.*

⮱**special** — *The CIA have special agents.*

⮱**suede** — *Sue loves suede.*

⮱**suppose** and **purpose**
*What do you sup**pose** is the pur**pose** of this **pose**?*
supp- *suppose, support, supper, supple — She's supple.*
purp- *purpose, purple*

⮱**teacher** — *The teacher teaches each student.*

⮱**their** — *He's **their** son and **heir**. It's **their heir**loom.
The inheritance is **theirs** because they are **heirs**.*

⮱**together** — *to get her. Let's go round **together to get her**.*

⮱**recovery** (re + cover + y) — *For a full **recovery**, you need to **cover** it.*

⮱**remember** — re + member — Remember all those e's.

⮱**young** — *You are so young.*

⮱**weird** — *We are weird.
We h<u>ire</u>d a bunch of we<u>ir</u>dos.*

Exercise 1

Can you see the word hidden in these words?

1. Connecticut — to join — _____

2. comparison — capital city — _____

3. sincerely — 5-letter word — _____

4. prevalent — an alcoholic drink — _____

5. pronunciation — in a religious order — _____

Thanks to Murray Suid: *Demonic Mnemonics*

Exercise 2

How many words can you find in these words?

1. cardigan (4 words) — _____

2. fortunate (4 words) — _____

3. management (5 words) — _____

4. transportable (6 words) — _____

Thanks to bbc.co.uk/skillswise

Exercise 3

Find the body parts. Each word has a body part, but one word has two body parts.

alarm, diagnose, friendship, merchandise, obeyed,

potatoes, searching, slippers

Thanks to Johanna Stirling's *Teaching Spelling*

Answers Exercise 1

Can you see the word hidden in these words?

1. **Connec**ticut — to join — <u>connect</u>

2. com**paris**on — capital city — <u>Paris</u>

3. **since**rely — 5-letter word — <u>since</u>

4. prev**ale**nt — an alcoholic drink — <u>ale</u>

5. pro**nun**ciation — in a religious order — <u>nun</u>

Answers Exercise 2

1. cardigan — *car, card, dig, an*

2. fortunate — *for, fort, tuna, ate*

3. management — *man, age, manage, men, gem*

4. transportable — *ran, port, transport, tab, table, able*

Answers Exercise 3

Find the body parts. Each word has a body part, but one word has two body parts.

al<u>arm</u>, diag<u>nose</u>, friends<u>hip</u>, merc<u>hand</u>ise, ob<u>eye</u>d, pota<u>toes</u>, s<u>ear</u>ching/sear<u>chin</u>g, sl<u>ip</u>pers

Thanks to Johanna Stirling's *Teaching Spelling*

Words-Within-Words Exercise

Underline the "hidden" word and then write it out.
e.g. Underline an animal in **edu<u>cat</u>ion** — <u>cat</u>

1. Underline something that's not true in **believe** _____

2. Underline a past tense verb meaning end of life in **studied** _____

3. Underline a type of metal in **environment** _____

4. Underline the final part in **friend** _____

5. Underline a part of the head in **learn** _____

6. Underline a number in **money** ____

7. Underline another word for everything in **usually** ____

8. Underline another word for hello in **while** ____

9. Underline a three-letter verb in **because** _____

Thanks to Johanna Stirling's *Teaching Spelling*

Answers

1. Underline something that's not true in bel**ie**ve — <u>lie</u>

2. Underline a past tense verb meaning end of life in stu**died** — <u>died</u>

3. Underline a type of metal in envi**ron**ment — <u>iron</u>

4. Underline the final part in fri**end** — <u>end</u>

5. Underline a part of the head in l**ear**n — <u>ear</u>

6. Underline a number in m**one**y — <u>one</u>

7. Underline another word for everything in usu**all**y — <u>all</u>

8. Underline another word for hello in w**hi**le — <u>hi</u>

9. Underline a three-letter verb in beca**use** — <u>use</u>

Exercise

Which is correct? Use your visual memory or your knowledge of words-within-words to help.

1. a. piece   b. peice

2. a. seperate   b. separate

3. a. because   b. becuase

4. a. friend   b. freind

5. a. envirament   b. environment

6. a. sincerly   b. sincerely

7. a. permunent   b. permanent

8. a. dilemma   b. dillema

9. a. persistent   b. persistant

10. a. Their son   b. They're son

11. a. Can you hear me?   b. Can you here me?

12. a. arguement   b. argument

13. a. acheivement   b. achievement

14. a. remember   b. remmember

Answers

1. a. piece ~~b. peice~~
2. ~~a. seperate~~ b. separate
3. a. because ~~b. becuase~~
4. a. friend ~~b. freind~~
5. ~~a. envirament~~ b. environment
6. ~~a. sincerly~~ b. sincerely
7. ~~a. permunent~~ b. permanent
8. a. dilemma ~~b. dillema~~
9. a. persistent ~~b. persistant~~
10. a. Their son ~~b. They're son~~
11. a. Can you hear me? ~~b. Can you here~~
12. ~~a. arguement~~ b. argument ~~me?~~
13. ~~a. acheivement~~ b. achievement
14. a. remember ~~b. remimember~~

Write your words-within-words, memory tricks, notes, thoughts, drawings...

Which is correct?

1. a. truely b. truly
2. a. becuase b. because
3. a. miniscule b. minuscule
4. a. necessary b. neccessary
5. a. accomodation b. accommodation
6. a. vanila b. vanilla
7. a. occasion b. ocassion

Answers on the next few pages.

42

Troublesome Letters

Focusing on the specific letters of words that cause problems brings your awareness to the source of the mistake, and helps you to commit the proper spelling to memory.

esl.dictionary

Most people usually know the beginnings and endings of words, and understand those patterns (*-ation, -ary, -ness, -ing*). It's the individual letters within a word that usually cause problems, especially single or double letters in words like *embarrass, necessary,* and *accommodate.*

Link the word to a relevant saying or rhyme, with the tricky letters making up the saying, like in the word-within-words strategy. If you don't understand a memory trick I've used, then spend some time working it out — this will help you study the word and learn it. Better still, make up your own tricks — it's fun, and you'll remember them.

---

forty = 40

No 'u' in forty

*There's a **u** in **four** and **fourteen** but u can't be **forty** (fou̶rty).*

or

***Forty** soldiers stormed the **fort**.*

➲ because   **because**

see the -au- in bec**au**se   **a**lways **u**nderstand
Because you need to always understand.

Or remember a word-in-the-word like in because — **use**
*Use this bec**au̲s̲e̲** then you'll **a̲**lways **u̲**nderstand.*

➲ **restaurant** — *The restaurant has a **rest**ful **aura**.*

➲ **truly** — **true** (drop the 'e') + **ly** = **truly**
*It's **truly** hot in **July**.*

➲ **minuscule** — This word comes from **_minute_** (tiny), so m̲i̲n̲u̲s̲cule.

➲ **Tuesday** — *Tuesday is bluesday.*

43

➲ **necessary/unnecessary**

Use sayings to help with the difficult 'c' and 's' letters.

It's neCeSSary to have 1 Collar and 2 Sleeves.

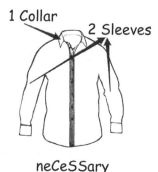

1 Collar

2 Sleeves

neCeSSary

or *It's neCeSSary to Cut Some Services.*

➲ **accessory** (two c's and 2 s's)

A Charming Chain in Shiny Silver <u>or Y</u>ellow gold is a good aCCeSS<u>ory</u>.
Accept the accessory.
accessories (change the **y** to **ies**)

Also *accessorise* (BrE) or *accessorize* (AmE and BrE).

➲ **occasion** (2 c's and 1 s)

On special oCCaSions I have Coffee, Cream and Sugar.

Also, *occasional occasionally*
occasion + al = *occasional* + ly = *occasionally*

Write your thoughts and memory tricks here.

'ass' Words

assistant — *The assistant is an ass.*
An ass and an ant are my assistants.
assassin — *An assassin is a double ass.*
harass — *He's an ass and crass to harass.*
embarrass — *I go really red and so shy when I'm embarrassed and feel like an ass.*

↪ **embarrass/embarrassed/embarrassing/embarrassment**
Tricky: double 'r' and double 's'

She has really red cheeks because she's Seriously Shy
and embarrassed

Do you go really red and Smile Shyly when you're embarrassed?

↪ **harass/harassment**
(*Don't get *harass* confused with *embarrass**)
Just one 'r' and double 's'
Ha, how crass to harass.
You don't have the right to harass, you ass!

↪ **trespass** — *Do not pass, you ass, or you'll trespass.*

→ Think of some suitable 'ass' sentences for these words:

assistant	*assault*	*associate/association*
assassin	*assignment*	*assume* *trespass*
harass	*assembly/assemble*	*embarrass*

⊃ **Caribbean** (1 r and 2 b's)
See the words within words: Carib bean, Ca rib be an
*There are really **b**eautiful **b**eaches in the Ca**rib**b**e**an.*

⊃ **receive** ("i before e except after c") *It's better to **g**i**v**e than recei**v**e.*

⊃ **perseverance**
*If you have per**sever**ance you are willing to do something **several** times before you get it right.*

⊃ **kindergarten** — *Teach **art** in kinder**ga**rten.*
"kin-der-gar-ten"

⊃ **knowledge** — *Know**ledge** is **power** and gives you the **edge.***

⊃ **millennium, millennial** (double 'l' and double 'n')
From Latin for thousand *mille*
Breaks down into syllables well: mil-len-ni-um, mil-len-ni-al

⊃ **murmur** — "**Mur**der, **mur**der," **murmur**ed the crowd.

⊃ **laugh** — *La**ugh** a**nd** yo**u** **g**et **h**appy.*

⊃ **occurred** — *The **c**ar **c**rash o**cc**u**rr**ed in a h**urr**y.*
occur**rence** — *I dread the o**cc**u**rr**ence of a **c**ar **c**rashing and **r**unning right into my **fence*** (a bit long, but I need to remember the –ence ending somehow). Can you think of a better sentence?

*The **c**able **c**ar a**cc**ident o**cc**u**rr**ed in a h**urr**y.*

Also see the double 'r' pattern in

occur	*recur*	*blur*
occurring	*recurring*	*blurring*
occurred	*recurred*	*blurred*

(More info about this doubling up rule in the Spelling Rules section)

⟳ accommodation(s)/accommodate(s)/accommodating

accommodate — drop the 'e' and add 'ion' or 'ions' = *accommodation(s)*
accommodate — drop the 'e' and add 'ing = *accommodating*

---

accommodation is chiefly British, and one of the most misspelled words.
accommodations is chiefly American.

Look at this photo I took in Yorkshire, UK, of a lovely hotel overlooking the sea.
Unfortunately, they didn't check the spelling, and neither did the signwriter.
They spelled it like they said it.

Use syllable breakdown: ac-com-mo-da-tion but this won't work if you
think it's spelled like it is in the above photo.

The problem with this word is usually with the **c's** and **m's**.

Better still, use a memory trick and sentence linked to *accommodation.*

*The a**cc**o**mm**odation has 2 **C**ots and 2 **m**attresses.*
*The a**cc**o**mm**odation has 2 **C**ribs and 2 **m**attresses.*

Don't forget the 2 o's — 2 r**O**und babies.
*Now that we have twins, our a**cc**O**mm**O**dation needs two **C**ots and two*
***m**attresses for our 2 r**O**und babies.*

Or
*The a**cc**o**mm**odation has 2 **c**ats and 2 **m**ice.*

More tricky **mm**'s. Notice these have a **mm + vowel**

➲ **dilemma** — *Emma is in a dilemma.*

➲ **flammable** — *Grass gets flammable in summer.*

➲ **immediately** = immediate + ly

 I ate my meal immediately.

 I ate the m & m's® immediately.

There are some double m's when adding the prefix –im to a root word beginning with 'm': im + mature = *immature* im + migrant = *immigrant immaterial, immeasurable, immodest, immobile...*

We'll see double 'm' in the 1:1:1 doubling up rule in the spelling rules chapter: swim — *swimmer, swimming, swimmable.* slim — *slimmer, slimming, slimmest.*

-comm- + vowel

➲ **committee**   committee

 Many meetings take time — everyone's exhausted.

committee, coffee, settee

➲ **communicate/communication** — *Mass media is now our communication.*

➲ **community** — *A summer community.*

➲ **commission** — *Come to the mission.*

➲ **comma** — *Comma errors are common.*

➲ **command** — *A comma commands space.*

➲ **commend** — *He was commended for his mending.*

 recommend (re + commend) = recommend, recommendation, recommending

-com- + p words

Notice these 'comp' words have one **m**.

They easily break down into syllables.

➲ **competition** — com-pe-ti-tion

 compete — com-pete

➲ **complete/incomplete** — com-plete — in-com-plete

 completely/incompletely — com-plete-ly, in-com-plete-ly

➲ **complain** — com-plain

➲ **comparison** — *Paris is beyond comparison.*

➲ **compatible, incompatible** — in-com-pa-ti-ble

➲ **competent, incompetent** — in-com-pe-tent. He's an incom**pet**ent pet owner.

➲ **complacent** — com-pla-cent

➲ **complex** — com-plex

➲ **complexion** — *I have a complex complexion.*

'h<u>app</u>y' Words

I'm **happy** it **happ**ened.

apparently — *My <u>parents</u> are **app<u>arent</u>ly** happy about the **rent**.*
appearance — *Your **app<u>earance</u>** at the <u>dance</u> made him **happy**.*
appetite — *I'm happy my <u>pet's</u> **app<u>eti</u>te** is back.*
appointment — *The <u>point</u> is to have a **happy app<u>oint</u>ment**.*
appreciate — *I **appreciate** being **happy**.*
appropriate — *The apple I <u>ate</u> was **appropri<u>ate</u>**.*
approve/approval — *I <u>value</u> their **app<u>roval</u>**, which makes me **happy**.*

dis + app
disapprove, disapproval
disappoint, disappointed, disappointment
disappear, disappeared, disappearance

A quick review exercise

1. a. unnecessary b. unneccessary

2. a. accomodate b. accommodate

3. a. aparently b apparently

4. a. miniscule b. minuscule

5. a. becuase b. because

6. a. liason b. liaison

7. a. committee b. commitee

8. a. immediately b. immedietely

9. a. Carribbean b. Caribbean

10. a. kindergarden b. kindergarten

Write a sentence with some of these troublesome words.

Answers: 1. a 2. b 3. b. 4. b 5. b 6. b 7. a 8. a 9. b 10. b

First Letters

Make up a saying where the first letter of each word in the sentence is one of the letters of the word. If it's related to the meaning, all the better.

because

big elephants can always understand small elephants

Or: *be ever careful and use sharp eyes*

big

elephants

can

always

understand

small

elephants

chaos

cyclones, hurricanes and other storms = chaos

---

diarrhoea (British English)

dash in a real rush, hurry or else accident

Or, *dining in a rough restaurant: hurry or expect accidents!*

diarrhea (American English)

dash in a real rush, hurry else accident

Or, *Dining in a rough restaurant: hurry, expect accidents!*

---

laugh — *laugh and you get happy.*

Wednesday — *We do not eat soup day.*

biscuits — *I love biscuits crumbled up into tiny pieces.*

---

rhythm

Say this sentence to yourself when spelling it *"rhythm has your two hips moving."* I use this all the time; it takes some effort to remember these, but it's worth it.

rhyme — *rhyme helps your memory expand*

Exercise

Which is correct? Use your visual memory, memory tricks and words-within-words to help you. If you're not sure, that's fine, look back over the words and tricks.

1. a. harrass   b. harass

2. a. tommorrow   b. tomorrow

3. a. dillema   b. dilemma

4. a. supercede   b. supersede

5. a. minuscule   b. miniscule

6. a. asignment   b. assignment

7. a. appointment   b. apointment

8. a. apparently   b. apparantly

9. a. completely   b. commpletely

10. a. comittee   b. committee

11. a. ecstacy   b. ecstasy

12. a. occurred   b. ocurred

13. a. unneccessary   b. unnecessary

14. a. forty   b. fourty

15. a. acknowledge   b. acknowlege

16. a. rythmn   b. rhythm

Answers

1. a. harrass b. harass

2. a. tommorrow b. tomorrow

3 a. dillema b. dilemma

4. a. supercede b. supersede

5. a. minuscule b. miniscule

6. a. asignment b. assignment

7. a. appointment b. apointment

8. a. apparently b. apparontly

9. a. completely b. commpletely

10. a. comittee b. committee

11. a. ecstacy b. ecstasy

12. a. occurred b. ocurred

13 a. unneccessary b. unnecessary

14. a. forty b. fourty

15. a. acknowledge b. acknowlege

16 a. rythmn b. rhythm

Spotting Vowels

In this section, we'll look at the importance of seeing vowels, especially in words like *sep<u>a</u>r<u>a</u>te, def<u>i</u>n<u>i</u>tely, relev<u>a</u>nt,* and *cemetery.*

We'll also go over some of the other words and strategies we've seen so far.

Spotting vowels is a great strategy for people with dyslexia. According to beatingdyslexia.com: 'Vowels are harder to clearly define than consonants. The vowels can cause greater confusion due to the variety of ways the letters can represent the sounds. This is why focusing on only the vowels can make spelling easier.'

---

www.beatingdyslexia.com/vowel-lessons.html

Focus on only the vowels: When I'm learning to spell a new word, the first thing I do is focus on only the vowels. I remember misspelling the word "sentence." If we look at only the vowels in the word "sentence", we can see they are all **e**'s:

s**e**nt**e**nc**e**

Sometimes, the meaning of a word can give us a clue to the vowel letter patterns.

beech or beach?
A b<u>ee</u>ch is a tr<u>ee</u>.   A b<u>ea</u>ch is by the s<u>ea</u>.

A cal<u>e</u>nd<u>a</u>r is a list of **dates.**
H<u>ear</u> with your **ear** and **learn.**
Do you bel<u>ie</u>ve a **lie?**

➔If you have problems with these words, use different colours (BrE)/colors (AmE) to highlight the vowels.

➔Can you see the vowels in these words?

cemetery
people
independent
irresistible

---

cemetery — *A cemetery is eerie with lots of greenery.*

independent/independence, sentence, tendency, recent, theref<u>o</u>re, exper<u>i</u>ence, extreme, ex<u>i</u>stence, remember,

unpre<u>c</u>edented/pre<u>c</u>edented (see the e's and hear the c)

Also e's in September: Sep-tem-ber
December: De-cem-ber

discipline (notice all those i's) discipline

people peOple pe ple

irresistible ir-res-is-ti-ble
Your new lip<u>st</u>ick makes you irresistible.

separate sep-a-rate or *Separate a rat.*   grammar

liaise, liaison li<u>a</u>ise, li<u>a</u>is<u>o</u>n   d<u>e</u>finit<u>e</u> — d<u>e</u>finit<u>e</u>ly
liaison — live in an igloo, **son**

visible *2 i's (eyes) are visible.*

significant significant   sign if I cant ("Sign if I can't.")

qualification qua-li-fi-ca-tion

mus<u>eu</u>m   Notice the 'u' either side of the 'e'?
See **use** in museum. *Use the museum.*

queue Four vowels in a queue! queue
Sue is blue stuck like glue in a queue.
(*line* in American)

various i.o.u various gifts I o (owe) u (you)

weird — Well weird!

Exercise. Fill in the missing vowels.

pe__ple, l__a__son, s__nt__nc__, gr__mm__r, w__ird

S__pt__mb__r, r__m__mb__r, D__c__mb__r, m__se__m

s__tisf__ct__ry, q__e__e, c__lend__r, __xp__ri__nc__

Check your spelling on this page and on the previous one.

-ie- or -ei- Patterns

Using the memory trick rhyme: "i before e except after a long c", is great for remembering some of the -ie- and -ei- words like *receive, achieve, receipt, ceiling*. But this famous saying is only for words that have a long "cee" sound: *receive, receipt, ceiling*.

> **-ie- patterns — "ee" sound — "i before e"**
> *achieve, mischief, mischievous, believe, relief, achievable, unbelievable, piece, niece, field, chief, thief...*
> Also: *priest, siege, hygiene, cashier, pier, shriek, diesel*

> **-ei- patterns — "ee" sound — "i before e except after a long c"**
> *receive, receipt, ceiling, conceive, deceit...*
> Also: *weird, Sheila, Keith, caffeine, protein, seizure, seize*

> **-ie- patterns — "shun" sound — "i before e when c is a 'sh' sound"**
> *ancient, patient, proficient, proficiency, efficient, efficiency, conscience*

> **-ei- patterns — "ay sound" — "i before e except when sounded like "ay" as in *neighbour* (BrE)/*neighbor* (AmE) and *weigh*"**
> *neighbour/neighbor, weigh, eight, freight, beige, veil, vein*

There are 8 sounds for -ie- and -ei- patterns:
1. the "ee" sound as in 'green' (*relief, field, receive, weird, mischievous*)
2. the "ay" sound as in 'pay' (*weigh, eight, vein*)
3. the "i" sound as in 'hit' (*foreign, counterfeit, sovereign*)
4. the "eye" sound (*height, feisty*)
5. the "eh" sound as in 'best' (*leisure, friend*) (*leisure* can be an "ee" sound in some American accents.)
6. the "shun" sound (*patient, ancient*)
7. the "oo" sound as in 'shoe' (*view, review, in lieu*)
8. separate sounds — variety, reinforce, quiet, fiery

→ You might not remember the rules but see the patterns instead, or use rhyming to help if you know how to spell one of these patterns.
-**iece**: *piece, niece*
-**ierce**: *fierce, pierce*
-**ield**: *field, yield, shield, wield*
-**ief**: *belief, relief, brief, chief, grief, thief, mischief*
-**ieve**: *believe, relieve, achieve, grieve, retrieve, thieve*
-**cei**: *conceit, deceit, receipt*   -**ceive**: *receive, conceive, deceive*

➔ Use memory tricks and words-within-words:
A piece of pie. Never believe a lie. It's a relief to lie down.
We are weird.

Exercise 1. Which one is correct and why? Does it follow a rule? Can you see the patterns to help?

1. a. recieve   b. receive

2. a. ancient   b. anceint

3. a. niece   b. neice

4. a. mischeivous   b. mischievous

5. a. reciept   b. receipt

6. a. achieve   b. acheive

7. a. peice   b. piece

8. a. believe   b. beleive

9 a. relief   b. releif

10. a. concieve   b. conceive

Check your spellings on the previous page.

Exercise 2. Fill in the missing -ei- or -ie-

anc__nt,   pat__nt,   profic__nt,   effic__nt,

w__gh,   __ght,   v__l,   n__ghbour/n__ghbor,   h__ght

v__w,   rev__w

rec__ve,   rec__ving,   rec__ved

bel__ve,   bel__ving,   bel__vable,   unbel__vable

ach__ve,   ach__vable,   ach__ving,

rec__pt,   conc__t,   conc__ve, dec__t,   dec__ve

ch__f,   bel__f,   rel__f,   th__f,   gr__f

misch__f,   misch__vous,   misch__vously,   misch__vousness

Check your spellings on the previous page.

Look, Say, Cover, Write, Check Method

Using this method is great because it makes you use various senses and actions — seeing the word, hearing it, thinking about it, visualizing it, and writing it.

It really improves your spelling if you use it every day. All you need is a pen and a piece of paper or notebook.

1. Write the word (or even a sentence) on a piece of paper, making sure you spell the word correctly.

2. **Look** at the word carefully — really study it. Any problem letters? Any familiar letter patterns? Any silent letters? Any prefixes, suffixes, root words?

3. **Say** the word out loud a few times. Does it break down into syllables? Any sounds similar to other words you know?

4. **Cover** the word. Say it again and form a visual image of the word.

5. **Write** the word. Don't worry about mistakes.

6. **Check** your spelling with the original. Check it carefully, letter by letter. Underline any mistakes and correct them. Think about why you made the mistake and any tricks to help you remember the correct spelling.

7. If incorrect, do these steps again until correct.

8. Repeat these steps after ten minutes, then after a day, then after a week.

Check out my video for more info in the Lessons section: www.howtospell.co.uk/LSCWvideo.php

Look, Say, Cover, Write, Check

Think about your mistakes — what are they? Why do you think you've made them? Keep doing this method every day. It's important to make sure you check your spelling letter by letter. Some people rush through, thinking they're right, but have missed a vital letter. This method works if you do it a little bit every day.

Write the word here. Check to see if it's spelled correctly!	achieve	believe	necessary	
Write the words downwards so you can check letter by letter	acheive			
Think about any mistakes and do the LSCW again a few times every day	achieve ✓			

Silent Letters — Their History and Rules

> *know, two, Wednesday, eight, knee, write, listen, could, walk...*
> All these common words have silent letters in them.
> ➜ Can you remember why we have silent letters?

More than 60% of English words have silent letters in them, which can cause all sorts of problems spelling them, pronouncing them, or looking for them in a dictionary.

Little Dinosaurs!
Silent letters are fossilized dinosaurs of a once-spoken letter, so let's look at their history and some rules.

One of the most useful strategies to improve spelling is knowing why we spell words the way that we do (the etymological system). Etymology is the study of the origin and history of words, and can be a great help when trying to understand spelling. Knowing why we have so many words with silent letters in them will not only help your spelling, reading, and pronunciation, but stop you getting frustrated with spelling.

English writing and spelling developed from the languages of the invaders that settled in England. Each time the country was invaded, so too was the English language and its spelling.

The first inhabitants we know of were the Celts (origins unknown). They spoke Celtic, which is still spoken and written in Scotland, Ireland and Wales. After them came:

43 AD — the **Romans** from Italy (Latin)

410 AD — the **Angles**, **Saxons**, and **Jutes** from Germany and Holland
　　　　　(Dutch/Germanic)

793 AD — the **Vikings** from Denmark and Norway (Old Norse)

1066 AD — the **French** (Norman French)

In 43 AD, the Romans invaded and colonized Britain. They spoke Latin. We still use some Roman Latin words. Look at these with silent letters in them: *scissors, salmon, debt, receipt, plumber.*

410 AD, the Anglo-Saxons

The Romans withdrew from Britain, and the **Anglo-Saxons** invaded from Germany and Holland. These Saxons, Angles and Jutes spoke a number of Germanic languages (west Germanic and Dutch) that eventually became Anglo-Saxon — **English!**

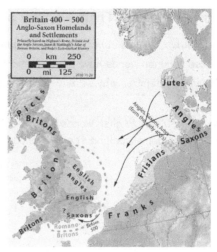

The 100 most common words in present day English are from Anglo-Saxon, including everyday words: *earth, house, food, sing, night, daughter, women, light, cough, sleep...*

The history of –gh-

The -gh- words are Anglo-Saxon.

daughter (*dohtor*), night (*niht*), light (*liht*), bright (*beorht*), dough (*dāg*), bough (*bōh*), rough (*ruh*), brought (*brohte*)

- The 'h' in the original spelling was a hard, throaty sound, like the Scottish sound in *loch*.

- Around the 13th century, 'g' was added to 'h', becoming 'gh', due to the French influence to try to spell this throaty sound.

- In about the 17th century, the 'gh' sound became silent: *night, daughter, though, through, plough, borough, slaughter.*

  Or, became the "f" sound: *enough, cough, tough, rough, laugh...*

We have a voiced gh- ("guh") at the beginning of words, but this pattern was introduced much later by Dutch/Flemish-influenced printers: *ghost, ghastly, ghetto, gherkin, Ghent...*

-gh- letter pattern word search.

Words can also be upside down, vertical, horizontal, backwards

bright
cough
eight
though
high
light
~~night~~
through
right
rough
thigh
tough
weight

```
r a e r t r h u h j b z j t y q e a h r
a v i k j h g i d g o r h p w t h g i r
w m g z e q u m a e u o i e n t o a w r
y s h j r p o x o z u o i g h c l g j x
k l t u y p r c l g j g r i h f x f m u
q c d k g a h d h e h u g d c t y b w i
d z s g e u t z v t r h t u j j d o l x
f n j d s l l p n w y b l i a r m a z a
b n u r x z z v q i k i e z s a o w x w
b s s n b g y a l q j c d y n t f h u b
e e j x w q u m z b l l z c v y g i a r
z v w d s q q l f c r p i h j i o t k p
n i g h t m q b v i o f u g h m k d g t
w h h j f u g m b s i w i a h g p s n h
j d b g w t f e i h w v y m g t f e s x
j o k s l c t q o n g c a s t w u i j b
j h l c w o k n u a n u t l g j z z f b
l i h l u i h p k c h a o h l s q v y k
l e v g e d i y z g r e y c q r s y c d
z g h e m r k i g w p l z t a h i e n p
```

793 AD, the Vikings

The Vikings from Denmark and Norway invaded.
They gave English lots of words, including the
silent letter words: *knife, knock, knee, knit, knuckle
gnat, gnaw, gnash...*

The silent **k** and **g** used to be pronounced, but in the 17th century began to drop
out of fashion.

The Saxon and Viking languages became Old English (sometimes referred to as
Anglo-Saxon).

1066 AD, the Norman French

The Norman French invaded in 1066 and at the Battle of Hastings conquered the Saxons. French and Latin became the language of law and the ruling classes for 300 years! Anglo-Saxon (English) was spoken by the peasants and the lower classes. English survived!

The French gave us an enormous vocabulary of words, but they changed a lot of our spellings to fit in with theirs.

-gu-

The French put a silent **U** in words like **guess** because in French **g** followed by **e** would sound like "j." So -gu- made it a "k" sound: *guide, guess, guilty, guard, guarantee, dialogue...*

gest (Old English) to **gu**est   vage (Old English) to vague

tunge (Old English) to ton**gu**e   voge (Old English) to vogue

But –gu- in these Latin/French words are a "gw" sound
anguish, distinguish, extinguish, languish, linguist

The Letter H

The pronunciation of the letter **h** in some words can be silent or pronounced, depending on your accent. For centuries, this letter wasn't pronounced, especially when the words came from French: *habit, history, honest, hospital, hotel...*

By the 18th century, **h** began to be pronounced in some words but not others. H was silent in *habit, harmonious, heritage, heir, herb, honest, humour/humor* and certain other words. Some of these words are now pronounced with the **h** in some accents.

Words that still have a silent **h** of French origin include: *heir, honest, honour* (BrE)*/honor* (AmE)*, hour, herb* (in AmE only). This is useful to know, because when you write *a* or *an*, you add *an* for a silent 'h'. *In an hour's time.*
A *historical* event but *an honest* approach.

1400s, Printers and Spelling

William Caxton and the printers of the 1400s altered spelling. Caxton lived many years in Flemish countries and introduced the Flemish way of spelling words with a gh: *ghost, ghastly, gherkin, ghetto.*

Some of the printers were Dutch and would spell words the Dutch way. An example of this was *yacht*. It was 'yott' before it was altered.

Academics and Silent Letters

The academics of the Renaissance in the 16th century were very enthusiastic about Classical Latin and Greek, which they thought of as intellectual. They wanted to imitate some Latin spellings to give English spellings more authority, so they shoved in those troublesome silent letters!

- **Doubt** (silent b) is a mix of Old French *doute* and Latin *dubitare*.
- **Debt** (silent b) is from the Latin *debitum*.
- **Subtle** (silent b) is from the Latin *subtilem*.
- **Receipt** (silent p) is a combination of Anglo/Norman French *receite* and Latin *recepta*.
- **Scissors** (silent c) was *sisoures*, but then a c was added because of the Latin *scindere*, to split.
- **Salmon** (silent l) was *samon*, then they added the silent 'l' to show its classical roots.

These words were originally spelled logically before the academics messed about with them and increased their complexity! The dictionary writers in 1830 agreed with these Renaissance fellows and left the silent letters in the spellings. They also didn't care whether spelling was easy or not, they just wanted it to reflect its Latin/Greek/French roots.

They sometimes increased the number of irregular forms: the Old English **gh** of *night* and *light* was added to *delight* and *tight*.

They borrowed words from these languages to express new concepts: *chaos, democracy, encyclopedia, pneumonia*.

Another three reasons why silent letters are in words:
1. Silent letters help the reader to recognize the difference between homophones: *knot/not, to/too/two, know/no, **whole/hole**, **write/right**...*

2. A silent letter can help us work out the meaning of the word and can change the pronunciation, even though it's silent: *sin/sign*, and the important silent 'e' to make a long vowel sound in *rat/rate, mad/made*.

3. Most of the pronounced silent letters became silent over the centuries, but the letters were left in the spellings because printing had fixed them.

Pronunciation always changes. Even now, we shorten words, slide letters together, chop letters off — all to make speaking easier, and a nightmare for spelling!

Memory Tricks and Strategies

Wednesday

Relying on pronunciation won't help with Wednesday. We say "wensday" with two syllables and a silent **d** and **e**. We can use syllable breakdown to help. Break the word down slowly and exaggerate the syllables when writing it — "Wed" "nes" "day". This helps you remember the silent 'd' and 'e' (more details in the Syllable section).

Or remember Wednesday is from Old English Wōdnesdæg 'day of Woden'.

island — *An island is **land** surrounded by water.*
write — *Write Words.*   **right** — right **h**and
mortgage to remember the silent 't', remember it's from Old French, literally meaning 'dead pledge', from **mort** (from Latin mortuus 'dead') + **gage** 'pledge' (from *Oxford Dictionary Online*).

<u>Words-within-words</u>

business — *Going by **bus** is good for **bus**iness.*
listen — *Please **list**en to the **list**.*

<u>See links between words</u>

***know** — knowing — knows — knowledge — knowledgeable — acknowledge*
***two** — twelve — twenty — twins — twice — twelfth — between*
***sign** — signal — signpost — signing — signature — signify — resign — resigning — resignation*

See the patterns and write sentences with them.
guitar, guilty, guide, guidance, fruit juice
I only play the guitar when drinking fruit juice in a suit.

light, right, bright, flight, sight, might, fright
I had a fright last night when my light went out.

More on these letter patterns, letter pattern stories, word families and word links in later sections.

Silent letter rules preparation
➔ Can you see the rules in these words?

write, wrong, wreck
knife, knock, knee
crumb, lamb, comb
palm, calm, salmon
walk, talk, yolk
damn, autumn, column

Silent Letter Patterns and Rules

kn- silent **k** before **n**: <u>kn</u>ee, know, knife, knives, knob, knobbly, knot, knuckle, knock, knack, knave, knead, kneel, knew, knit...

gn- silent **g** before **n**: gnat, gnaw, gnash, gnarl, gnome...

-gn- align, assign, benign, design, malign, reign, sign, campaign, poignant, champagne, cologne, foreign...

wr- silent **w** before **r**: <u>wr</u>ite, wrist, wrinkle, wring, wriggle, wrong, wrote, wrap, wreck, wrench, wrestle (silent w, t, e)

ps- silent **p** before **s**: <u>ps</u>ychic, psalm, psychology, psychiatry...

-lk silent **l** before **k**: fo<u>lk</u>, walk, talk, yolk, chalk...

-mb- silent **b** after **m**: plu<u>mb</u>er, numb, dumb, thumb, crumb, climb, limb, lamb, succumb, bomb, comb, tomb, womb...

-mn silent **n** after **m**: autu<u>mn</u>, column, solemn, condemn, damn, hymn...

-lm- silent **l** before **m**: palm, calm, psalm (silent p & l), qualm, alms, almond, balm, salmon...

-st- silent **t** after **s**: li<u>st</u>en, fasten, glisten, moisten, hasten...

-stle bristle, bustle, castle, gristle, hustle, jostle, mistletoe, rustle, thistle, whistle, wrestle (silent w/t)

The silent **l** in three important words: would, could, should

Write some silent letter pattern stories. If you know how to spell one of these words, then it might help you spell the others in the pattern.

The plumber climbed the old tomb but it crumbled, and he broke his thumb, which now felt numb.

I tried to knead the knot out of the knitting but didn't know how, so I cut it with a knife but cut my knuckle instead.

Write a couple of silent letter pattern sentences.

Silent to Sounded

Consonants that are silent in some words are sometimes pronounced/sounded in a related word; for example, the **g** in *sign* is silent but voiced in *signal* and *signature*. This is probably to aid pronunciation.

When the silent letters are sounded, they are voiced in a separate syllable: "**sig**-nal", "**sig**-na-ture", "re-**sig**-na-tion", "ma-**lig**-nant", "crum-**ble**", "bom-**bard**", "mus-**cu**-lar", "con-dem-**na**-tion".

The sounded consonant can help you spell, or remember, the related word with a silent letter.

silent — pronounced/sounded/voiced

bomb — bombard, bombardment
limb — limber
crumb — crumble, crumbling
condemn — condemnation
damn — damnation
solemn — solemnity
Christmas — Christ
fasten — fast
hasten — haste
moisten — moist
soften — soft, softly
muscle — muscular
malign — malignant
design — designate
resign — resignation
sign — signal, signature
knowledge — acknowledge

Careful:
numb/number (no feelings): *My numb thumb is number than before.*
The 'b' in *numb* and its comparative adjective *number* are silent.

number/numbers (1, 2, 3, 55, 76...) But we have the voiced **b** in *number* 1 or *numbers.*

Exercise.

We have some silent letters in some body parts.

---

1. Write in the missing letters.

a: __nee   b: __rist   c: pa __m   d: shou __der

e: thum_____   f: mus__les

---

2. Write in the missing words.

1. This is a _____

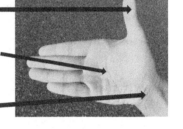

2. This is the _____ of the hand.

3. This is a _____

4. This is a _____

5. He's building up his _____.

Answers

1. a: <u>k</u>nee   b: <u>w</u>rist   c: pa<u>l</u>m   d: shou<u>l</u>der   e: thum<u>b</u>   f: mus<u>c</u>les

2.

1.   This is a <u>thumb.</u>

2.   This is the <u>palm</u> of the hand.

3.   This is a <u>wrist.</u>

4.   This is a <u>knee.</u>

5.   He's building up his <u>muscles.</u>

In the next chapter, we're going to look at homophones

➔ Look at this sentence:

Please send me a peace of you're work.

All the words are spelled correctly so the spellchecker on your computer won't give you a red line underneath them. But two words are wrong. If you have a spellchecker that has a grammar check, then these two words will have squiggly blue lines underneath them.

➔ Correct the two words that are wrong.

The sentence should be: *Please send me a **piece** of **your** work.*

Sound-Alikes — Homophones

*there/they're/their, to/too/two, right/write, been/bean
witch/which, bye/buy/by, here/hear, it's/its, pear/pair/pare
new/knew, piece/peace, genes/jeans, here/hear...*

homophones = words that have the same sound but
different meanings and different spellings.

homophone comes from the Greek words:
homos = same + *phone* = sound

I want to buy that pear. **or** *I want to buy that pair.*
Thinking allowed. **or** *Thinking aloud.*
I rode around the lake. **or** *I rowed around the lake.*

If you write, 'We need too right a letter,' the spell-checker will not detect a misspelling. In terms of writing done on a computer, such homophone errors are the most common type of misspelling, sometimes the only type you might see in a word-processed document.

One way to avoid these misspellings is to be aware of the most common homophones and proofread carefully when using them. Work on the ones that confuse you the most, and if in two weeks you can thoroughly remember the difference between three or four homophone errors, that would be an important victory.

Professor Larry Beason: *Eyes before Ease*

Using memory tricks to help you figure out which homophone is which is so important. I use strategies like seeing words-within-words, and memory trick phrases to help me, especially when I go over my work to check if I've used the correct word.

People from every walk of life, regardless of their educational level and background, make mistakes when spelling words such as *principle* and *principal*, *desert* and *dessert*, *stationery* and *stationary*, as well as dozens of other every day, same-sounding words, i.e. homophones.

http://www.4sliteracy.com.au/publications14.asp

Homophones are tricky because the computer won't necessarily tell you if you've used the wrong one. In the exercise below, my computer grammar-check is indicating (with a blue squiggly line) that four common homophones are wrong, but it hasn't given me any indications that a further seven are also wrong. That's why proofreading even the shortest of emails, and going over every piece of writing, is so important. I've made errors thanks to predictive text, too.

- Read everything carefully before you press send.
- Read it aloud and slowly to see if you've missed any small words, endings, or punctuation.
- Read the notoriously tricky homophone words again (use spelling strategies ~~too~~ check ~~weather there wright. x~~) (use spelling strategies to check whether they're right).

You should go over every single word and sentence you type, not only because of predictive text but because, when you type fast, the first homophone that pops in your head will usually be the one you type, especially when you want to get your feelings and thoughts out urgently and without thinking about spelling.

Be very mindful of homophones and use tricks to help you see if you've used the correct one.

Using visual clues, memory tricks, dictionary definitions, and sentences will help you learn these words and hopefully write them automatically.

The context of the word can help you decide which homophone should be used. For example, *a home can be for sale*, while *a boat can have a sail*. Or we may need more information: *I want to buy that pear* or *I want to buy that pair*. A juicy pear to eat, or a pair of shoes?

Exercise. Proofread these sentences and correct the homophones.

1. We'll go threw it again after we take a brake and have a peace of cake.

2. I'm hear to wright a report.

3. You're car is blocking mine.

4. What's going on over their?

5. My son needs some stationary for college.

6. Do you know were there from?

Using memory tricks to help you remember which word is which is one of the best strategies to help you. When you use a memory trick, especially words-within-words, it's best if you link the difficult bits with something connected with the word's meaning.

➔ Let's look at some very common homophone mistakes, and possible memory tricks to use.

---

peace/piece
Can you remember the word within the word in *piece*?

⇨ This is a **pie**ce of **pie**.
  There's a pie in piece.

⇨ Pe**ace** is **ace**.
  Peace of mind is ace.
  *Pe*a*ce *a*nd love are so peaceful.*

---

brake/break
⇨ *Jake had to brake suddenly to avoid an accident.*
  *Jake's car br*a*ke pads were f*a*ke.*
⇨ *You **break** your night **fast** at breakfast.*
  ***Eat** a **steak** for breakfast.*

bra**ke**

---

through/threw
⇨ *I **threw** the new ball* (**threw** is the past of **throw**).
  *He **threw** it **through** the window.*
⇨ *We walked **through** the park and then **through** town.*

---

write/right
⇨ ***Write Words***

*I need to **Write Words** right when **Writing**.*
*writing — drop the 'e' with -ing writ*e ➔ *writing*

⇨ **right** = correct ✓ or turn right, right hand.
  *I write with my rig**ht** h**and**.*

> **wright** is an archaic word for maker or builder. We still see it in *playwright*.

hear/here

⇨**here** = place

Remember the **here** in these words about place:
There, where, everywhere, nowhere.
Where is it? It's here!

⇨Remember the word within **hear** that relates to hearing:
Hear with your ear and learn.
hear, hears, hearing, heard

See the **ear** letter pattern in this sentence
(remember letter patterns can have different sounds):
The bear likes to wear earrings on each ear.

---

your/you're

⇨**your** = possession: my, his, her, your, their, **our** house, **your** house.
  See the **our** in y**our**.
  This is **ours**. That is y**ours**.
⇨**you're** is the short form/contraction of *you are.*
  The apostrophe replaces the 'a' and joins the two words together.

you're = you are

→ *Do you like your work? or Do you like you're work?*

  Do you like your work? √ To see if it's right, swap the *your* for *my* or *our*
— Do you like my/our/your work? √
But *Do you like **you're** work? = Do you like **you are** work?* is wrong.

---

there/their/they're

⇨**there** = place = *here, t**here**, w**here**, there is, there are, there was, there were, is there/are there?*
⇨**their** = possession = *my car, their car. The**ir** — I = my — their*
⇨**they're** is a contraction of *they are,* so when reading your work back, say *they're* as *they are* and you'll soon see if it's correct.

they're = they are

where/were/we're

⇨ **where** = place and relates to *here, there, where*
Also, *where is/are/was/were*

⇨ **were** is the past tense of *are*: *you/they/we were, were you/they/we?*

⇨ **we're** = we are   **We're** *(We are) going to the park.*

Where were you yesterday? The kids **were** looking forward to seeing you.
*I don't know **where** they **were** last night.*
*I don't know **where** they are today.*

stationery/stationary?

⇨ Station**e**ry = **e**nvelopes pens, paper...
Station**ery** = pap**er**

⇨ Station**a**ry = at the station, a station**a**ry c**a**r, stationary in a traffic jam.

Station**e**ry = **e**nvelopes
Station**a**ry = c**a**rs

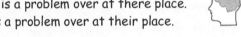

→Which is correct?

1. a. There is a problem over at they're place.
   b. They're is a problem over at there place.
   c. There is a problem over at their place.

2. a. They were going over there.
   b. They where going over there.
   c. They we're going over there.

3. a. Let's take a brake and go somewhere peaceful.
   b. Let's take a break and go somewhere pieceful.

4. a. I walk through the park every day.
   b. I walk threw the park every day.

5. a. He had to brake suddenly to avoid hitting a stationery car.
   b. He had to brake suddenly to avoid hitting a stationary car.
   c. He had to break suddenly to avoid hitting a stationary car.

6. a. I hope you're right about it.
   b. I hope your right about it
   c. I hope you're write about it.

Answers

1. a. ~~There is a problem over at they're place.~~
   b. ~~They're is a problem over at there place.~~
   c. There is a problem over at their place.

2. a. They were going over there.
   b. ~~They where going over there.~~
   c. ~~They we're going over there.~~

3. a. Let's take a brake and go somewhere peaceful.
   b. ~~Let's take a break and go somewhere pieceful.~~

4. a. I walk through the park every day.
   b. ~~I walk threw the park every day.~~

5. a. ~~He had to brake suddenly to avoid hitting a stationery car.~~
   b. He had to brake suddenly to avoid hitting a stationary car.
   c. ~~He had to break suddenly to avoid hitting a stationary car.~~

6. a. I hope you're right about it.
   b. ~~I hope your right about it.~~
   c. ~~I hope you're write about it.~~

→ **Preparation Exercise.** Which is correct?

1. a. You're not **allowed** to go in there.   b. You're not **aloud** to go in there.
2. a. They have two **groan** children.   b. They have two **grown** children.
3. a. I don't know **whether** to go or not.   b. I don't know **weather** to go or not.
4. a. Mrs Smith is a school **principal**.   b. Mrs Smith is a school **principle**.
5. a. I love delicious **deserts**.   b. I love delicious **desserts**.
6. a. I **guessed** you had a **guest**.   b. I **guest** you had a **guessed**.
7. a. What's your **waist** size?   b. What's your **waste** size?

---

aloud/allowed

⇨ *You are so loud so stop talking aloud.*
⇨ *Will we be allowed in?*

*If y**ou** keep on talking **aloud**, you wi**ll** not be **allowed** to stay.*

---

grown/groan

⇨ *I'm all **grown** up and can stay home on my **own**.*
⇨ *To **moan** and **groan** is so annoying.*

weather/whether

⇨ *You can only **eat** outside in good **weather**.*
⇨ ***Whet**her we like it or not, we are part of a global economy.*
Why? When? What? Whether or not?
***Whether** or not the **weather** is good or **whether** it's bad, we'll go.*

Poem
Whether the weather is fine,
Whether the weather is not,
We must weather the weather,
Whatever the weather,
Whether we like it or not.   Anon

principle/principal

⇨ The *principle* rule.

⇨ *The school princi**pal** is not your **pal**.*
  *I have a **pal** who's a princi**pal** deputy on the munici**pal** council.*

desert/dessert

⇨*De**s**ert is **s**and.*
⇨*De**ss**ert is **s**weet **s**tuff.*

guest/guessed

⇨**guest** *She's a touri**st** and gue**st**.*
⇨**guessed** is the past tense of to **guess**
I guessed it right. She/He/They/We/You guessed

waist/waste

⇨ *I have a 22-inch waist.*
*The **wai**ter has a narrow **waist**.*
⇨ *I hate waste. Don't **waste** the **paste** in **haste**.*

Answers

1. a. You're not **allowed** to go in there. b. You're not aloud to go in there.
2. a. They have two groan children. b. They have two **grown** children.
3. a. I don't know **whether** to go or not. b. I don't know weather to go or not.
4. a. Mrs Smith is a school **principal**. b. Mrs Smith is a school principle.
5. a. I love delicious deserts. b. I love delicious **desserts**.
6. a. I **guessed** you had a **guest**. b. I guest you had a guessed.
7. a. What's your **waist** size? b. What's your waste size?

Exercise

1. We had lunch over at _____ house. (there/their/they're)

2. _____ are you from? (Where/Were/We're)

3. I always walk _____the park to get to work. (through/threw)

4. I _____ what he wanted. (knew/new)

5. _____ grandmother used to live over _____. (their/there/they're)

6. I hope _____ _____lots of people at _____ party.
   (there/their/they're, where/we're/were, your/you're)

7. _____ not thinking about _____ future because _____
   too young to care. (there/their/they're)

8. _____ going to the beach today. (Where/We're/Were)

9. I hope _____ phone's OK and you _____able to phone home.
   (you're/your, where/we're/were)

10. The train was _____ outside the station for 30 minutes.
    (stationery/stationary)

11. The _____ gave all the staff a _____ of cake.
    (peace/piece, guessed/guest)

Exercise

1. We had lunch over at **their** house.

2. **Where** are you from?

3. I always walk **through** the park to get to work.

4. I **knew** what he wanted.

5. **Their** grandmother used to live over **there**.

6. I hope **there were** lots of people at **your** party.

7. **They're** (They are) not thinking about **their** future because **they're** (they are) too young to care.

8. **We're** (We are) going to the beach today.

9. I hope **your** phone's OK and you **were** able to phone home.

10. The train was **stationary** outside the station for 30 minutes.

11. The **guest** gave all the staff a **piece** of cake.

What are the homophone partners to these words? Some have two or three possible partners.

aisle — _____   allowed — _____

aren't — _____   ate — _____

days — _____   dear — _____

die — _____   praise — _____

swayed — _____   brews — _____

board — _____   loan — _____

Check on the next page.

Common Homophones List

Look in your dictionary and find the meanings of the words you don't know.

➜ Some of these might not be homophones in your accent.

aisle / I'll / isle
allowed / aloud
aren't / aunt
ate / eight
ball / bawl
band / banned
bare / bear
be / bee
bean / been
blew / blue
board / bored
brake / break
bred / bread
brews / bruise
brows / browse
buy / by / bye
caught / court (British)
ceiling / sealing
cell / sell
cent / scent / sent
cereal / serial
check / cheque (British)
chews / choose
coarse / course
claws / clause
cue / queue (British)
currant / current

days / daze
dear / deer
dew / due
die / dye
died / dyed
draft / draught
fair / fare
farther / father
find / fined
flaw / floor
flew / flu / flue
flour / flower
for / fore / four
formerly / formally
genes / jeans
grate / great
groan / grown
guessed / guest
heal / heel / he'll
hear / here
heard / herd
he'd / heed
hi / high
higher / hire
hour / our
knew / new
knot / not
know / no
knows / nose

lacks / lax
licence / license (British)
links / lynx
loan / lone
made / maid
mail / male
mane / main
meat / meet
meter / metre
missed / mist
morning / mourning
one / won
owed / ode
past / passed
paste / paced
pair / pare / pear
pause / paws / pores / pours
pawn / porn
pea / pee
peace / piece
phrase / frays
place / plaice
plain / plane
please / pleas
praise / prays / preys

rain / reign / rein
raise / rays / raze
rap / wrap
raw / roar
right / rite / write
road / rode
role / roll
root / route (British)
rose / rows
sail / sale
saw / soar / sore
scene / seen
sea / see
seam / seem
seas / sees / seize
sight / site
sighs / size
sighed / side
sew / so / sow
some / sum
son / sun
stair / stare
stationary / stationery
steal / steel
storey / story
swayed / suede
tale / tail
tacks / tax
teas / tease
there / their / they're
threw / through
throne / thrown
tide / tied
to / too / two

waist / waste
wait / weight
war / wore
way / weigh
weak / week
we'd / weed
weather / whether
were / where / wear
which / witch
wine / whine
who's / whose
wood / would
word / whirred
worn / warn
your / you're

➔ If you don't understand a word,
check in a dictionary (list of the good
ones in the back).

Past simple/participle homophones — regular (-ed endings)

allowed / aloud	guessed / guest
banned / band	leased / least
balled / bawled / bald	mined / mind
based / baste	missed / mist
billed / build	mowed / mode
bored / board	owed / ode
bussed / bust	packed / pact
brewed / brood	passed / past
crewed / crude	towed / toad / toed
cited / sighted / sited	tied / tide
died / dyed	seemed / seamed
fined / find	soared / sword

Past simple/participle homophones — irregular

ate / eight	read / red
been / bean	rode / road
blew / blue	rose / rows
bred / bread	saw / sore
caught / court *not in American	seen / scene
fought / fort	sent / cent / scent
flew / flu	sold / soled
grown / groan	sought / sort *not in American
heard / herd	taught / taut
knew / new	threw / through
made / maid	thrown / throne
mown / moan	wore / war
	worn / warn

Exercise 1

Write in the homophone for these words ending in **s**. Most of their homophone partners don't end in **s**. Example: brews — <u>bruise</u>
Some of these might not be homophones in your accent.

1. chews _____

2. claws _____

3. brows _____

4. knows _____

5. days _____

6. frays _____

7. who's _____

8. prays _____

9. rays _____

10. pleas _____

11. teas _____

12. sighs _____

13. tacks _____

14. sees _____

Exercise 2

Which homophone goes with these regular past tense words? Notice the -ed endings either have a "t" or "d" sound. For example, *allowed* — <u>*aloud*</u> *missed* — <u>*mist*</u>

1. banned _____

2. billed _____

3. brewed _____

4. owed _____

5. mowed _____

6. bawled _____

7. swayed _____

8. missed _____

9. guessed _____

10. weighed _____

11. soared _____

12. packed _____

13. tied _____

14. paced _____

Exercise 3. Which homophone goes with these irregular past tenses?

1. ate _____

2. sought _____ (not in some accents)

3. made _____

4. knew _____

5. heard _____

6. bred _____

7. rode _____

8. threw _____

9. worn _____

10. thrown _____

11. blew _____

12. been _____

13. seen _____

14. grown _____

Proofread this famous poem by Jerrold H. Zar, from 1992. The spellchecker won't find anything wrong with this!

Eye have a spelling chequer,

It came with my Pea Sea.
It plane lee marks four my revue

Miss Steaks I can knot sea.

Eye strike the quays and type a whirred

And weight four it two say

Weather eye am write oar wrong

It tells me straight a weigh.

Eye ran this poem threw it,

My chequer tolled me sew.

Possible Answers Exercise 1

1. chews — <u>choose</u>
2. claws — <u>clause</u>
3. brows — <u>browse</u>
4. knows — <u>nose</u>
5. days — <u>daze</u>
6. frays — <u>phrase</u>
7. who's — <u>whose</u>
8. prays — <u>praise</u> or <u>preys</u>
9. rays — <u>raise</u>
10. pleas — <u>please</u>
11. teas — <u>tease</u>
12. sighs — <u>size</u>
13. tacks — <u>tax</u>
14. sees — <u>seas</u> or <u>seize</u>

Answers Exercise 2

1. banned — <u>band</u>
2. billed — <u>build</u>
3. brewed — <u>brood</u>
4. owed — <u>ode</u>
5. mowed — <u>mode</u>
6. bawled — <u>bald</u> or <u>balled</u>
7. swayed — <u>suede</u>
8. missed — <u>mist</u>
9. guessed — <u>guest</u>
10. weighed — <u>wade</u>
11. soared — <u>sword</u>
12. packed — <u>pact</u>
13. tied — <u>tide</u>
14. paced — <u>paste</u>

Answers Exercise 3

1. ate — <u>eight</u>
2. sought — <u>sort</u>
3. made — <u>maid</u>
4. knew — <u>new</u>
5. heard — <u>herd</u>
6. bred — <u>bread</u>
7. rode — <u>road</u>
8. threw — <u>through</u>
9. worn — <u>warn</u>
10. thrown — <u>throne</u>
11. blew — <u>blue</u>
12. been — <u>bean</u>
13. seen — <u>scene</u>
14. grown — <u>groan</u>

Answers Proofreading Exercise

(**The original version**) Eye have a spelling chequer,
It came with my Pea Sea.
It plane lee marks four my revue
Miss Steaks I can knot sea.

Eye strike the quays and type a whirred
And weight four it two say
Weather eye am write oar wrong
It tells me straight a weigh.

Eye ran this poem threw it,
My chequer tolled me sew.

***

➔ <u>**The corrected version**</u>
I have a spelling checker,
It came with my PC.
It plainly marks for my review
Mistakes I cannot see.

I strike the keys and type a word
And wait for it to say
Whether I am right or wrong
It tells me straight away.

I ran this poem through it,
My checker told me so.

Visual Spelling Patterns

Good spellers see letter patterns, links, and relationships between words. Knowing common letter patterns is a reliable way to help spelling.

> There are some strings of letters which occur very often. Good spellers are able to remember these easily and can visualise the letter patterns in words.
> Basic Skills Agency: *Starter Pack*

> *It is only through **visual** familiarity with language that you can learn about the probable spelling of words. Spelling is about visual sequences of letters.*
> Sue Abell: *Helping Adults Spell*

Good spellers have an excellent visual memory for what looks right. They know the beginning "kw" sound in *qualification* is spelled with **qua** like the other **qua** words, such as *quarter, quantity, quaint, quality...*

They know that the suffix ending that sounds like "shun" is either: -tion, -sion or -cian. If they spell *quolificasion* like this, they can usually see that this looks wrong.

You can develop this skill, too, by practising (BrE)/practicing (AmE) spelling and noticing the patterns and rules. Spelling won't happen by just reading about it — you have to study it, notice it, work at it, and use it.

The pattern might make different sounds in different words. It's more about developing your visual memory for what looks right.

-eigh- *eight, height, weight, freight, neighbour* (BrE)/*neighbor* (AmE)
-ank- *sank, bank, thank, tank, blank, Hank*
-ink- *sink, pink, think, stink, blink, chink*
br- *brick, bridge, bright, brandy, brilliant*
gr- *green, grass, grate, great, gracious*

Identifying Letter Patterns

Letter patterns are also called letter strings.

-ight	-tch	pl-	spr-	br-	pr-
light	match	play	spring	brown	prince
bright	watch	plan	sprung	bring	princess
might	hutch	plenty	sprat	brunt	price
uptight	notch	plank	sprog	Britain	prank

According to Johanna Stirling: There are certain letter patterns that occur so often that we need to be able to write them automatically as "chunks" of spelling, rather than letter-by-letter. For example:

beginning patterns: st-, br-, pl-, bl-, gl-, thr-, spr-, sk-

end patterns: -nt, -ed, -ful, -ness, -sure

vowel patterns: ou, ow, ie, ei, oy, igh, ough, au

consonant patterns: ng, th, ch, sh

It's important to start "really" seeing words, noticing patterns and thinking about words that are linked by letter pattern. Good spellers see these patterns, links, and understand relationships between words, and the exceptions.

How can letter patterns help with spelling?

When you're spelling it helps to remember letters as a group or pattern rather than remembering each letter on its own. For example: -**ough** is found in the words *through* and *enough*.

You only need to learn to spell a letter pattern once to help you spell lots of different words that have the same pattern.

Letter patterns are especially useful in English because English words are not always spelt the way that they sound. This means we can't always rely on the sounds of letters to help us spell or read. For example: -**tion** sounds like *shun*.

http://teach.files.bbci.co.uk/skillswise/en20memo-11-f-what-are-letter-patterns.pdf

Sounding Out and Visual Memory

A lot of letter patterns can be put into sound groups, which means we can rhyme an unfamiliar word with a possible letter pattern.

So rhyming a word with another word that has the same letter pattern is a great strategy to help you recall spellings, and to see how the word might be written. But there are often exceptions that you need to learn too. Look at these examples; they have the same patterns but with some sound exceptions:

found, pound, round but *young*

eight, weight, weigh but *height*

autumn, August but *Australia*

how, now, cow but *blow, know*

match, batch, hatch but *watch*

soon, moon, tycoon but *book, took*

Now look at these words with the same sound but different letter patterns to see how developing your visual memory for what looks right is important.

believe, achieve but *receive*

Light, flight, right, bright slight but *write, site, kite*

air, hair, flair, affair but *hare, flare, aware, care*

plain, train, vain, rain but *plane, lane, vein, reign, champagne*

Rhyming a word can offer clues or even very clear indications of likely letter patterns if we know all the possible variations.

Common errors

---

think or **thing** — *I **think** I understand everything now, except this **thing.***

-**ink**: *think* — to think = verb. *I think I need a drink!*
ink, think, pink, drink, rink, sink, blink, slink, brink, wink, mink...

-**ing**: *thing* — a thing = noun. *That ring thing is so bling.*
ping, ring, sing, bling, swing, wing, ting, zing...
One-word pronouns: *everything, something, nothing, anything*

---

than or **then**
*It's much bigger **than** I thought, but **then** again it's cheaper than the smaller one.*

than — *can, tan, flan, ban, pan...* comparative adjective — *bigger than. I'm happier than, taller than, more than...*
then — *ten, hen, pen, men, when, send in Ken then Ben then Len,*
then *this happ**en**ed, then this, then that...*

Initial Letters

str- *street, strip, stripe, strap, straight, strength...*
scr- *scrap, scrape, scream, scrub, scrutiny...*
spr- *spring, sprint, sprinkle, sprocket...*
sp- *spit, spot, spat, spoon, spacious*
st- *stint, stop, stunt, stance, standard*
sn- *snip, snob, snap, snatch, snoring*
sc- *scare, scale, scowl, school, scallop*
sl- *slip, slap, slob, slipper, slippery*
pl- *play, place, plate, plane/plain, plentiful*
bl- *blue, black, blow/blew, blimey*
pr- *print, prod, predict, princess, prince*
br- *bring, brand, brought, bright, brilliant*
cr- *cream, crease, crinkle, crazy, crept, crank*

➜ Make a letter pattern dictionary and add more words and patterns.

---

brought and bought

Do you get these confused?   Memory trick

Remember: *brought* is the past of **bring**   bring — brought
               bought is the past tense of **buy**.

I brought (bring) *a cake to work that I bought at the deli.*
He bought some flowers and brought (bring) *them to work.*

Exercise

Write in the initial letter patterns

1. First meal of the day = ____eakfast

2. The part of the head that thinks = ____ain

3. What you need when you are thirsty = ____ink

4. It's nice on apple pie = ____eam

5. The day before Saturday = ____iday

6. When a floor is wet, it becomes ____ippery

7. This is a ____aight line   ━━━━━━━━

8. The past tense of *bring* is ____ought

Answers

1. First meal of the day = **breakfast**

2. The part of the head that thinks = **brain**

3. What you need when you are thirsty = **drink**

4. It's nice on apple pie = **cream**

5. The day before Saturday = **Friday**

6. When a floor is wet, it becomes **slippery**

7. This is a **straight** line ━━━━━━━━━━

8. The past tense of *bring* is **brought**

Write a sentence with as many initial letter patterns as you can.

Exercise

Add **than** or **then, brought** or **bought, think** or **thing**

1. It's bigger _____ I expected. (than/then)

2. What do you _____ about the _____ he _____ from Amazon? (think/thing bought/brought)

3. I'll go to the baker and _____ I'll go to the post office. (than/then)

4. The _____ is, I didn't _____ you'd want to come. (thing/think)

5. She _____ it from the market and _____ it to work. (brought/bought)

Answers

1. It's bigger **than** I expected.

2. What do you **think** about the **thing** he **bought** from Amazon?

3. I'll go to the baker and **then** I'll go to the post office.

4. The **thing** is, I didn't **think** you'd want to come.

5. She **bought** it from the market and **brought** it to work.

Letter pattern dictionary and stories

To help you learn to spell these, you need to develop your visual memory for what looks right, and one strategy is to make a letter pattern dictionary and list the words by patterns, and also their sound groups. Then make letter pattern sentences or stories.

→ Next, we're looking at –**ant** or –**ent**. Can you see which is correct?

a. important or importent?

b. restaurant or restaurent?

c. independant or independent?

Check your answers on the next page.

-ant/-ent

These are tricky patterns because they sound alike, so let's use an *ant* and a *tent* as a memory trick.

-ant	-ent
 *This **ant** is eleg**ant** and pleas**ant** but not arrog**ant** or irrelev**ant**. Adam Ant was a pop star in the 80s. (Notice the play on the word adamant.)*	*Stud**ents** are cont**ent** to sleep in **tents** to be independ**ent** and differ**ent**.*
-tant *assistant, important, distant, hesitant, reluctant*	**-tent** *tent, content, discontented, instant, competent, consistent, persistent*
-rant *fragrant, ignorant, tyrant, currant, restaurant, warrant*	**-rent** *rent, parent, apparent, different, current*
-dant *attendant, redundant, abundant descendant*	**-dent** *evident, student, independent, resident, president, accident,*
-lant *jubilant, stimulant, plant, transplant*	**-lent** *lent, silent, violent, equivalent, excellent, repellent*
(hard **c** — "k" sound) **-cant** *vacant, scant, significant*	**-cent** (soft c — sound "s") *cent, accent, scent, recent, decent, innocent, magnificent*
(hard **g**) **-gant** *elegant, arrogant, extravagant*	**-gent** (soft g) *gent, intelligent, agent*

-ant/-antly/-ance/-ancy

→ Which **ant** are you?

eleg**ant**, import**ant**, pleas**ant**, toler**ant**, vibr**ant**,
exuber**ant**, observ**ant**, gall**ant**, relev**ant**, extravag**ant**,
brilli**ant**, vigil**ant**, abund**ant**, jubil**ant**, ench**ant**ed,
const**ant**, vali**ant**, observ**ant**, triumph**ant**

or

dist**ant**, domin**ant**, arrog**ant**, vac**ant**, flipp**ant**, hesit**ant**, ignor**ant**, reluct**ant**,
irrelev**ant**, resist**ant**, defi**ant**, repugn**ant**, stagn**ant**, nonchal**ant**?

Are you pregn**ant**, an account**ant**, a ten**ant**, an eleph**ant**,
a conson**ant**, an immigr**ant**, a restaur**ant**, a gi**ant**, a contest**ant**,
a tyr**ant**, an inf**ant**, a pl**ant**, a fragr**ant** vagr**ant**, an assist**ant**, redund**ant**?

→ Can you think of a memory trick for these? Or, break them into syllables or words-within-words.

→ Write 3 sentences.

Notice these patterns:

-ant	-antly	-ance	-ancy	-ate
arrogant	arrogantly	arrogance	--	--
relevant	relevantly	relevance	relevancy	--
irrelevant	irrelevantly	irrelevance	irrelevancy	
elegant	elegantly	elegance	--	--
abundant	abundantly	abundance	--	--
tolerant	tolerantly	tolerance	--	tolerate
tenant	--	--	tenancy	--
vacant	vacantly	--	vacancy	vacate
dominant	dominantly	dominance	--	dominate
hesitant	hesitantly	--	hesitancy	hesitate
significant	significantly	significance	--	--
extravagant	extravagantly	extravagance	--	--

We have some root words that just add the –ance ending:

perform — *performance*

avoid — *avoidance*

appear — *appearance*

annoy — *annoyance*

inherit — *inheritance*

insure — *insurance*

guide — *guidance*

account — *accountant, accountancy*

Drop the 'e' and add -ance:

observe — *observant, observance*

ignore — *ignorant, ignorance*

-ant and –ance / -ancy are used with hard 'c' and 'g' sounds:
elegant/elegance,
extravagant/extravagance,
significant/significance
vacant/vacancy

-ent/-ently/-ence/-ency

➔How differ**ent** are you?

> confid**ent**, excellent, magnificent, independ**ent**, intelligent, eloquent,
> silent, innocent, different, competent, resilient, patient, efficient,
> decent, persistent, talented, consistent, prudent, convenient, fluorescent
> or
> violent, decadent, disobedient, complacent, impatient, insolent, ardent?

Are you a resident, a correspondent, a patient, a client, a parent, a gent,
an agent, an adolescent?

➔See all the **e**'s in ind**e**p**e**nd**e**nt

➔Can you think of any memory tricks or word-within-word tricks for these?

lent —

dent —

cent —

rent —

tent —

gent —

➔Write some sentences.

I **reside** here so I'm a **reside**nt in this **reside**nce.

➔Who's resid**ent** in the **tent**?

The gent in the tent is a permanent resident.

-ent	-ently	-ence	-ency
different	differently	difference	--
resident	--	residence	residency
independent	independently	independence	codependency
efficient	efficiently	--	efficiency
silent	silently	silence	--
innocent	innocently	innocence	--
excellent	excellently	excellence	excellency
permanent	permanently	permanence	permanency

Notice the vowels and memory tricks:
excel — excellent — **excellence**
independent — independence
different — difference
The **man** is a per**man**ent resident in the tent
reside — resident — residence: **Sid** is a re**sid**ent on this **side** of the road.

-**ment** is a very popular suffix added to root words to form nouns to refer to a result of an action or process: *excitement, curtailment*, disappointment.

Some of them are in the commonly misspelled list: *argument, embarrassment, equipment, government, environment, harassment, parliament.*

Also: *management, apartment, assessment, cement, comment, compartment, document, entertainment, experiment, development, commitment, payment, employment, unemployment, sentiment, statement, supplement, torment, settlement, instrument...*

Keep the 'e' in
excitement, arrangement, advertisement, achievement, involvement, replacement, endorsement, management, pavement...

Exceptions: But drop the 'e' in argue + ment = *argument.* Can you remember the memory trick?

acknowledgement or *acknowledgment* are both acceptable but *acknowledgment* is chiefly used in American English.

Oxford Dictionary says: *In British English, the normal spelling in general contexts is* **judgement**. *However, the spelling* **judgment** *is conventional in legal contexts, and in American English.*

-ere to -rence / -rent	-er + -ence = -rence
revere — reverence / reverent	confer — conf**erence**
adhere — adherence / adherent	infer — *inference*
cohere — coherence / coherent	prefer — *preference*
interfere — interference	refer — *reference*
	transfer — *transference*
Exception: persevere — *perseverance*	differ — *difference*

If the root word ends in a soft 'c' and 'g' then the ending will be –**ence** or –**ency**.

adolescent — adolescence   decent — decency   urgent — urgency
    innocent — innocence   agent — agency   emergent — emergency
intelligent — intelligence   complacent — complacency
  negligent — negligence   proficient — proficiency
  indulgent — indulgence   efficient — efficiency
belligerent — belligerence — belligerency

Exception: **vengeance**

Word containing –**cid**-, -**fid**-, -**sid**- or -**vid**-, it'll be the -**ent**/-**ence** suffixes: *confidence (confident), evidence (evident), incidence (incident), residence (resident), providence (provident).*

Exercise. Change these words to -ence or -ance

1. perform — _____

2. intelligent — _____

3. guide — _____

4. differ — _____

5. confident — _____

6. ignore — _____

7. independent — _____

8. inherit — _____

9. ignore — _____

-ent word search

Word searches are good for developing your visual memory.

```
a t m p o y t g t c i t i r t
t z n c a n r n p n i n t e n
k n h e e r e o d q n e t c e
t i e d l n e e g o t l t e l
h n u u i l p n c q e o n n a
p t e t q e e e t b l i e t t
s j n l n e n c g l l v n e s
c o i d i t r u x g i w a f x
c l e b g s q f u e g y m f g
y n t n e t s i s r e p r i j
t c o n f i d e n t n x e c o
w t n e g r u g q n t v p i e
t w v d z b x i q r n c k e d
t n e d i c c a a n c i e n t
v j m r l d o m c i r e d t y
```

accident   recent
ancient   silent
confident   student
continent   talent
efficient   urgent
excellent   violent
frequent   intelligent
independent   parent
innocent   permanent
                  persistent

Exercise 1. Write in the **ent** or **ant** ending.

1. independ_____

2. assist_____

3. suffici_____

4. anci_____

5. import_____

6. perman_____

7. restaur_____

8. arrog_____

9. pregn_____

10. ineffici_____

11. abund_____

12. pleas_____

13. tal_____

14. viol_____

15. differ_____

16. confid_____

17. import_____

18. relev_____

Exercise 2. Write in the **ance** or **ence** ending.

1. independ_____

2. assist_____

3. arrog_____

4. import_____

5. perman_____

6. abund_____

7. sent_____

8. viol_____

9. experi_____

10. differ_____

11. confid_____

12. relev_____

Answers Exercise 1

1. independent (see all those e's)
2. assistant
3. sufficient
4. ancient
5. important
6. permanent
7. restaurant
8. arrogant
9. pregnant
10. inefficient
11. abundant
12. pleasant
13. talent
14. violent
15. different
16. confident
17. important
18. relevant

Answers Exercise 2

1. independence
2. assistance
3. arrogance
4. importance
5. permanence
6. abundance
7. sentence
8. violence
9. experience
10. difference
11. confidence
12. relevance

Notes

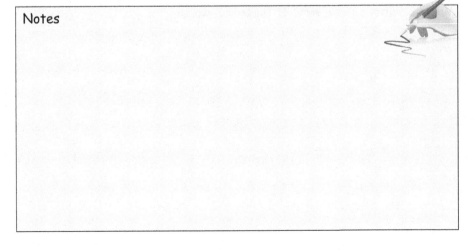

-ou- Pattern

-ound: *round, pound, sound, found, hound, bound, ground, mound...* If you have trouble spelling one on these, you can try rhyming, or use a letter pattern story rhyme:

"My hound found a round pound on the ground on top of a mound."

-ouble: *double, trouble*

-ouple: *couple*

-ouse: *house, mouse...* *"There's a mouse in my house."*

-our: *our, scour, flour, sour, devour...* But *your, four, pour, tour...*

-oud: *loud, proud, cloud...* *"He's loud and proud with his head in a cloud."*

-out: *out, outside, about, pout, spout, sprout...*

-outh: *south, mouth*

-ount: *count, mount, mountain, fountain...*

British/American
council/council
councillor/councilor
counsellor/counselor

Our house is your house.

young — See the *you* in *young* — **"You** are so **young."**

doubt *"It's natural to be in doubt."* This helps with the silent **b.**

Write a sentence with some of these -ou- words.

-ow- Pattern

-ow: *how now brown cow, brow, vow, wow, allow, bow**
"How now brown cow with a big brow."

-ow: *low, know, show, snow, grow, crow, bow**, glow, mow, stow, throw, flow, tow... "I know the snow is low but you can't mow."*

Combine them both: *"Now is the time to know how to grow and glow and vow to wow and throw those old low feelings out."*

-own: *brown, down, town, gown, clown, down, drown, frown...*
-owl: *owl, fowl, growl, howl, prowl, scowl...* But *bowl*
-ower: *flower, tower, power, shower...*

-ow at the end of words:
-low: *low, flow, blow, slow, below, bungalow*
-llow: *willow, follow, hollow, shallow, yellow, pillow, swallow,* but *allow*
-rrow: *arrow, sorrow, marrow, barrow, tomorrow*
-dow: *window, shadow*

Add more words to your letter pattern dictionary when you see these patterns.

Write a sentence with some of these -ow- words.

-igh- Pattern

Can you remember why we have this -gh- pattern?

The -ight- words are some of the most common words in English and trickiest to spell. We can use rhyming to help.

-igh: *high, sigh, thigh, higher*
-ight: *light, bright, delight, fight, flight, night, might, right, tight, eyesight, sightseeing...*

(Careful, we have the same sound in **-ite** words: *bite, site, kite, write.*)

-eigh: *eight, weight, weigh, neighbour/neighbor* (AmE)
but *height* has a different sound.

Letter pattern stories

Writing sentences or drawing pictures can plant the words and pattern into your memory.

It's good to have a bright light at night or your eyesight might not be right.

My friend took a flight to New York and went sightseeing, and was delighted to see the bright lights.

Let's look at some homophone words with **-ight** and **-ite**.
write/right — *I write with my right hand.*
You write words. See the 'w' in **write** words.
right and left. See the 'h' in right hand.

sight/site — *I went sightseeing but saw lots of building sites.*
sight, eyesight, sightseeing
building site, website, campsite
site is from Latin *situs* meaning local position.
sight is from Anglo-Saxon *sihth* meaning something seen. Remember "h" became "gh".

Write a sentence with some of these -ight- words.

The long "a" sound — "ay"

Vowel sounds can be spelled many different ways. We don't have enough vowels to account for all the different sounds we need in English so we pair up the vowels. This gets complicated because we also have different patterns for the same sounds.

The same "ay" sound occurs in the *-ay, -ai-, a-consonant-e* patterns, and some *-ey* and *-ei-* words. But the position of the pattern in the word determines the spelling.

Many scholars didn't like the letter 'y' in the middle of root words unless they were of Greek origin, so we have the root words *pay, say, stray,* with the 'ay' pattern coming at the end of words, and the *-ai-* pattern in *rain, plain, drain* coming in the middle of words just because the academics didn't like rayn, playn, drayn!

Magic 'e' — the silent 'e' at the end of words — is usually used to make long vowel sounds, including the "ay" sound in *crane, plane, pane, Shane.*

We also have -**ei**- making the "ay" sound, too, in *eight, neigh, weigh, weight, neighbour/neighbor, sleigh, freight, reindeer, beige.* There are only a few of these, so they can be memorized, or you can write a letter pattern story to help remember them:

Eight beige reindeer for my neighbour's/neighbor's sleigh were delivered by freight.

We also have -**ey** in *prey, they, hey, grey* (BrE)/*gray* (AmE)

We have some words where the -ai- is short and unstressed: *plaid, certain, said. Again* can be short or long.

More on short and long vowel sounds in the Phonic Strategies section.

Look at these with the same long "a" sound.

-**ay** at the end of single syllable root words	-**ai**- in the middle (never at the end)	**a_e** **a** + consonant(s) + magic e
ray	rain	crane
tray	train	trade
may	mail	male
X-ray	rail	rake
astray	available	evade
play	plain	plane
day	daily	dale
stray	strain	strange
way	wait	wave
pay	pain	pane
bay	bait	bathe
way	waist	waste
Jay	jail	Jane
stay	sail/ snail	sale / stale
say	said certain (short vowel sound)	sane

Exception: *maybe* (may + be) is a compound word from the old phrase *it may be (that).*

Add suffixes to -**ay** to change the grammar, and the position!
play — plays, played, playing...   *say — says, saying...*
pay — payable, payday, payload, paying...   *stay — stayed, staying, stays...*

Exercise with –ain-

Write the correct words in the gaps.

Spain, certain, train, rain, sprained, complained, maintain, explain,
explaining, detained, again, stained, chain, dainty

1. He fell down and _____ his ankle.

2. I'd better take an umbrella, it might _____

3. I _____ to the manager of the restaurant about the useless service.

4. I dropped a glass of red wine and _____ the carpet.

5. After the third time _____ about the loss of my gold _____ they asked me to _____ it all _____.

6. I had some cakes from the patisserie and they were so _____ and light.

7. The commuter _____ was so packed and hot, I felt dizzy and almost _____.

8. The man was _____ at customs on suspicion of smuggling.

9. I'm absolutely _____ we've met before.

10. Most people are finding it hard to _____ their standard of living.

11. She's British but she lives in _____.

Answers Exercise

*Spain, certain, train, rain, sprained, fainted, complained, maintain, explain,
explaining, detained, again, stained, chain, dainty*

1. He fell down and <u>sprained </u>his ankle.

2. I'd better take an umbrella it might <u>rain</u>

3. I <u>complained</u> to the manager of the restaurant about
   the useless service.

4. I dropped a glass of red wine and <u>stained</u> the carpet.

5. After the third time <u>explaining</u> about the loss of my gold <u>chain,</u> they
   asked me to <u>explain</u> it all <u>again</u>.

6. I had some small cakes from the patisserie and they
   were so <u>dainty</u> and light.

7. The commuter <u>train </u> was so packed and hot, I felt dizzy and almost
   <u>fainted.</u>

8. The man was <u>detained</u> at customs on suspicion of smuggling.

9. I'm absolutely <u>certain</u> we've met before.

10. Most people are finding it hard to <u>maintain</u> their standard of living.

11. She's British but she lives in <u>Spain</u>.

Look at these patterns and the position of them in the root word

-oy (end)	-oi- (middle)
toy	toilet
boy	boil
joy / enjoy	join / joint
ploy / employ	exploit / poison
-oy- is in the middle of a few words before a vowel royal loyal foyer voyage voyeur flamboyant	celluloid paranoid typhoid
Exception: oyster*	choir* sound difference

long "oo"

-ew-	-ue-	-ui- middle
blew	blue	bruise
dew	due	juice
stew	sue	suit
flew	flue	fruit

"oh" sound

-ow- (end)	-oa- (middle)
low	load
tow	soap
crow	coat
grow	goal
throw	toast

Some More Tricky Vowel Patterns

-au- Pattern
Autumn is a beautiful time when the leaves turn auburn.

autumn (*fall* in American English), **August**
Autumn comes after August.
In autumn, the leaves turn auburn.
auction, audible, auto, automobile, automatic
authentic, author, authorise/ authorize, authority
aunt, aunty, aura
haul, maul, Paul, Pauline
applause, cause, pause, nauseous, nausea
caught, taught, daughter, naughty, slaughter, haughty
caution, cautious,
sauce, saucepan, sausage,
laundry, faucet

With **restaurant** sometimes the –au- is unstressed or silent.
The restaurant has a restful aura.

Because you need to always understand.
Big Elephants Can't Always Understand Small Elephants.

Past tense words: *taught* (teach), *caught* (catch)

Letter pattern stories
I'm going for a walk with my aunty and daughter because it's a beautiful autumn day.
Paul, Pauline and their daughter felt nauseous after they caught flu off their aunty.

Now write a letter pattern story or sentence with –au-

Exercise with –au– word column

All the words contain the -**au**- pattern.

This helps your visual memory for what looks right.

---

1. A season __ __ __ __ __ __ in British English.

2. The month after July __ __ __ __ __ __

3. The past tense of *teach* __ __ __ __ __ __

4. I have two children, a son and a __ __ __ __ __ __ __ __

5. The past tense of catch __ __ __ __ __ __

6. Another word for very pretty __ __ __ __ __ __ __ __

7. Be careful = Be __ __ __ __ __ __ __ __

8. They write books __ __ __ __ __ __(s)

9. To stop for a moment __ __ __ __ __

10. P__ __ __ and P__ __ __ __ __ __ are my uncle and

   __ __ __ __ __

Answers

All the words contain the **-au-** pattern.

---

1. A season — **autumn**

2. The month after July — **August**

3. The past tense of *teach* — **taught**

4. I have two children, a son and a **daughter**.

5. The past tense of catch — **caught**

6. Another word for very pretty — **beautiful**

7. Be careful = Be **cautious**

8. They write books — **author**(s)

9. To stop for a moment — **pause**

10. **Paul** and **Pauline** are my uncle and **aunty** (or **aunt**)

-ui- Pattern
After our fruit juice, U and I need to pack our suitcases for our cruise to see the penguins.

Short sound:
build, builder, building "U and I build a house"
circuit, biscuit
guilt, guilty, guide, guild, guitar, guinea pig, guillotine, quit

Long "oo" sound: *juice, fruit, suit, suitable, suitcase, ruin, recruit, sluice, cruise, bruise*

Short Sound: *anguish, distinguish, extinguish, penguin, liquid, quit*

Long "eye" sound: *disguise, acquire, beguile,*
quite, quiet
Please keep quiet about my diet.

quit = short sound and one syllable. Add an 'e' and you get *quite* a long sound.
quite = long sound and one syllable
quiet = long sound and two syllables

homophones: suite / *sweet*

Letter pattern stories
A penguin in a suit stopped playing his guitar and started drinking fruit juice, but the penguin ruined his suit with fruit juice.
A bruise will ruin fruit.
I quit my job because it was quite stressful, now my life is quiet.

Now write a -ui- letter pattern story or sentence.

Word column with –ui–

This helps your visual memory for what looks right.
<u>Note</u> that the same letter pattern makes different sounds.

---

1. The opposite of innocent __ __ __ __ __ __

2. Squeeze an orange and you get this __ __ __ __ __

3. A matching jacket and trousers __ __ __ __

4. Someone who puts up houses __ __ __ __ __ __ __

5. Apples, pears, oranges, etc. __ __ __ __ __

6. A musical instrument with strings __ __ __ __ __ __

7. To give up, stop doing something __ __ __ __

8. To carry clothes in for holidays — luggage __ __ __ __ __ __ __ __

9. Another word for silent __ __ __ __ __

10. To put out a fire, cigarette, etc. __ __ __ __ __ __ __ __ __

11. To destroy, damage, spoil something __ __ __ __

12. To go on holiday and travel around on a ship __ __ __ __ __ __

13. When you bang yourself hard, you get this mark __ __ __ __ __ __

14. This black and white bird lives in Antarctica and can't fly

__ __ __ __ __ __ __

Answers

1. The opposite of innocent — **guilty**

2. Squeeze an orange and you get this — **juice**

3. A matching jacket and trousers — **suit**

4. Someone who puts up houses — **builder**

5. Apples, pears, oranges, etc. — **fruit**

6. A musical instrument with strings — **guitar**

7. To give up, stop doing something — **quit**

8. To carry clothes in for holidays — luggage — **suitcase**

9. Another word for silent — **quiet**

10. To put out a fire, cigarette, etc. — **extinguish**

11. To destroy, damage, spoil something — **ruin**

12. To go on holiday and travel around on a ship — **cruise**

13. When you bang yourself hard, you get this mark — **bruise**

14. This black and white bird lives in Antarctica and can't fly — **penguin**

-ea- Pattern

There are 8 sounds for -ea-

*I **hear** that an **early breakfast** of **beautiful peaches, pears** and **steak** is good for your **health** and **heart**.*

long e "ee": *sea, pea, tea, eat, meat, beat, heat, neat, seat, treat, breathe, clean, lean, mean, bean, bead, read, knead, plead, lead, seam, team, beam, steam, dream, cream, scream, stream, jeans, beak, leak, weak, peak, sneak, creak, squeak, heal, real, really, deal, meal, seal, steal, squeal, each, beach, peach, teach, reach, east, feast, beast, peace, tease, please, easy, season, leaf, leaves...*

short e: *head, bread, dead, tread, spread, death, breath, dread, deaf, wealth, health, read* (past tense), *lead* (metal), *breakfast, breath, sweat, ready, heavy, heaven, weather...*

long u "who": *beauty, beautiful, beautician...*

long "ear": *ear, near, hear, dear, year, fear, tear (cry), clear, beard, gear, smear, idea...*

long a sound "ay": *break, steak, great.* These 3 are the only common words with this sound.

r influenced long sounds
long "ar": *heart, hearth, hearty, heartfelt...*
long "er": *wear, bear, swear, pear, tear (rip)...*
long "ur": *early, earth, heard, learn, earn, search, pearl, rehearse, rehearsal, yearn...*

Exercise

1. Summer, autumn (fall), winter, spring are _____.

2. British people are obsessed with the _____ and always carry an umbrella with them.

3. My _____ is very good; I never go to the doctor's.

4. Google is a _____ engine.

Answers

1. Summer, autumn (fall), winter, spring are <u>seasons</u>.

2. British people are obsessed with the <u>weather</u> and always carry an umbrella with them.

3. My <u>health</u> is very good; I never go to the doctor's.

4. Google is a <u>search</u> engine.

Word column exercise with –ea-

1. We live on planet __ __ __ __ __

2. The past tense of *hear* __ __ __ __ __

3. When something or someone is very pretty

   __ __ __ __ __ __ __ __

4. This person's job is in a classroom __ __ __ __ __ __ __

5. The points of a compass are north, __ __ __ __, south and west.

6. 12 months = a __ __ __ __

7. To have lots of money means you're __ __ __ __ __ __ __

8. The opposite of strong is __ __ __ __ __

9. This is the first *meal* of the day __ __ __ __ __ __ __ __ __

10. The plural of *leaf* is __ __ __ __ __

11. Another word for *perspire* is __ __ __ __ __ __

12. You __ __ __ __clothes, you __ __ __ food, you __ __ __ __ books.

Answers

1. We live on planet <u>earth</u>.

2. The past tense of *hear* — <u>heard</u>

3. When something or someone is very pretty — <u>beautiful</u>

4. This person's job is in a classroom — <u>teacher</u>

5. The points of a compass are north, <u>east</u>, south and west.

6. 12 months = a <u>year</u>

7. To have lots of money means you're <u>wealthy</u>.

8. The opposite of strong is <u>weak</u>.

9. This is the first *meal* of the day — <u>breakfast</u>

10. The plural of *leaf* is <u>leaves</u>.

11. Another word for *perspire* is <u>sweat</u>.

12. You <u>wear</u> clothes, you <u>eat</u> food, you <u>read</u> books.

Write a letter pattern story or 3 sentences with as many -ea- words as you can.

-ea- word search

```
e u b y q z i l e a r n k t c r n d
d o g s s k b f r g r e f a e n t t
n z p h g a t a n r d d a h e n u a
p s i b e a e y c n q n c l t t b e
b d g r j a e t d j k a e t l n s r
w r i e a a v r w s e h q j e y k g
j e h h r m a y n t s e a s o n b c
a a l t c e l a e m c j y k x s e r
t m h a h f c x g g s y r o k h a s
n s n e c w t r a e h m r z k k u h
w s a w d c t b t i k t c f c p t v
i z q f r a k i i c s s d y s q y a
r o b e k i i g k a b y x z f l s t
j x a a i a p v r g c l p g z f d q
m m l s e z e m z m z w v f q y v q
y m f u a w l r j u f q g s y c c x
q t f j w j u t b p o e b s k n t q
y v z o l y k n f x u z l s d q o g
```

beauty	heard	meal	teacher
breakfast	heart	really	weather
cream	heavy	season	
dream	learn	steak	
earth			
easy			
great			

→ Next, we're going to look at some tricky letter patterns that come at the end of words: **-ate**, **-acy**, **-asy**, **-sede**, **-ceed**, **-cede** **-ary**, **-ery**, **-ory**

1. Some **-ate** words are stress shift words. Can you hear the pronunciation differences in this sentence? *It's hard to **separate** the **separate** bits.* (Check on the next page.)

2. *supercede* or *supersede*? (page 121)

3. What are the three words ending in **-ceed**? (page 121)

4. *ecstasy* or *ecstacy*? (page 121)

5. I need to buy some *stationary* or *stationery*? (page 123)

-ate

ate, hate, fate, gate, date, mate, plate, skate, state, later, relate, migrate, sedate, cheapskate, inflate, aggravate, concentrate, illustrate, translate, chocolate, climate, delicate, immediately, desperate, unfortunate, exhilarate, intimidate, sophisticated, accommodate, demonstrate, exaggerate...

Stress shift words

Look at the following words: *alternate, moderate, deliberate, estimate, elaborate, graduate, associate, delegate, certificate.* They are stress shift words, which means that they change stress and sound slightly differently depending on how we use the word.

Read this sentence: *It's hard to **separate** the **separate** bits.*

Notice how the –ate in "to **separate**" (verb) is more stressed than "the **separate** bits" (noun).

→ Verb: to "sepaRATE" (stressed) — *Can you separate them?*
→ Adjective: "SEPrut" (unstressed) — *It's a separate word.*

alternate (verb) / (adjective)
moderate (verb) / (adjective)
deliberate (verb) / (adjective)
estimate (verb) / (noun)
elaborate (verb) / (adjective)
graduate (verb) / (noun)
associate (verb) / (noun)
delegate (verb) / (noun)
certificate (verb) / (noun)

Knowing these stress shift words can help you with the spelling of them, especially the letter before the -ate, if the long verb versions slowly and exaggeratedly.

Write a letter pattern story or 3 sentences, for example, *I ate some delicate chocolate with my mate.*

Word Column

All the words contain the **-ate-** pattern

---

1. The past tense of eat: __ __ __

2. This is sweet and comes in dark or milk __ __ __ __ __ __ __ __ __

3. June 4th; 20th Feb; Wed, 6th May are all __ __ __ __ __ __

4. Another word for a friend __ __ __ __

5. To give a rough value, amount, and price of something:

   The builder gave me an __ __ __ __ __ __ __ __ *for the work.*

6. To say something is bigger, better, worse than it is

   __ __ __ __ __ __ __ __ __

7. To really focus on something and not get distracted

   __ __ __ __ __ __ __ __ __ __

8. Instant. Sudden. Occurring now.

   Take __ __ __ __ __ __ __ __ *action.*

Answers

1. The past tense of eat — <u>ate</u>
2. This is sweet and comes in dark or milk — <u>chocolate</u>
3. June 4th; 20th Feb; Wed, 6th May are all <u>dates</u>
4. Another word for a friend — <u>mate</u>
5. To give a rough value, amount, and price of something:
   The builder gave me an <u>estimate</u> for the work.
6. To say something is bigger, better, worse than it is — <u>exaggerate</u> .
7. To really focus on something and not get distracted — <u>concentrate</u>
8. Instant. Sudden. Occurring now.
   Take <u>immediate</u> action.

-acy and -asy

Nouns endings in -**acy** and -**asy** have the same sounds. The -acy words are more common.

-acy

-ate to -acy

privacy, immediacy, legacy, fallacy, lunacy, intimacy, delicacy, pharmacy

Change the -te to -cy

numera**te** — numera**cy**	delica**te** — delica**cy**	priva**te** — priva**cy**
pira**te** — pira**cy**	intrica**te** — intrica**cy**	intima**te** — intima**cy**
litera**te** — litera**cy**	adequa**te** — adequa**cy**	legitima**te** — legitima**cy**
accura**te** — accura**cy**	immedia**te** — immedia**cy**	

Change the -t to -cy

democra**t** — democra**cy**,

bureaucra**t** — bureaucra**cy**,

aristocra**t** — aristocra**cy**,

conspire — conspirator — conspira**cy**

-racy: *democracy, literacy, bureaucracy, piracy, accuracy, conspiracy, numeracy, aristocracy*

-macy: *primacy, pharmacy, supremacy, legitimacy*

-asy

There are only four words with **-asy**:
ecstasy, fantasy, idiosyncrasy, apostasy

ecstasy "ec-sta-sy" "ec-**sta**sy"
It has the same beginning sound as *extra,* so don't be confused and put 'x'.
It has the same sound and letter pattern as *echo.*
There are two s's — ec**s**ta**s**y. Don't forget the **s** after the **c**: ec**s**tasy.

Fill in the missing letters

ecst__ __ __,   __cst__sy,   ecsta__ __,   e__ __ __a__ __

fant__ __ __,   f__nt__y,   fanta__ __,   __a__ __a__ __

-sede, -ceed, -cede Patterns
These endings have the same sound. The *Oxford Dictionary* says: There are only ten verbs in common use with these endings but a lot of people have difficulty spelling them (*supersede, exceed, succeed, proceed, recede, concede, precede, intercede,* accede, secede).

-sede
supersede is the only word ending in **-sede.**
supersede, supersedes, superseded, superseding

It means *to replace* or *to take the place of* something/someone that is old, or no longer useful.
*Former stars were being **superseded** by younger actors.*
*Former stars were being **replaced** by younger actors.*

Notice all those e's and two s's: **super**sede

-ceed and -cede
Words ending in the same sound as **-sede** are **-ceed** and **-cede.**

➜ Only 3 words end in **-ceed**: *exceed, succeed, proceed*

-cede is the most common ending and some useful words are *recede, concede, precede, intercede.* Notice all the e's in these.

Fill in the missing letters

super__ __ __ __,   s__p__rs__d__,   __u__e__ __e__e

suc__ __ __ __,   s__cc__ __d,   __u__ __ee__

re__ __ __ __,   r__c__d__,   __e__e__e

121

-ary/-ery/-ory Patterns

These endings are tricky because they sound the same. They all come from Latin for "belonging to", "connected with", "having to do with (whatever it is affixed to)": *library, machinery, victory*

-ary Pattern

library (connected with books), *missionary* (belonging to a mission), *revolutionary, stationary* (originally meant belonging to a military station), *primary* (from Latin first), *dictionary* (manual or book of words), *vocabulary* (list of words)

Letter pattern endings: *-tary, -sary, -nary, -rary, -lary, -mary*

-sary: nece**ssary**, anniversary, glossary,

-rary: tempo**rary**, library, literary

-nary: extraordi**nary**, imaginary, stationary, dictionary, ordinary, missionary, revolutionary, legen**dary**, boundary

-mary: custo**mary**, primary, summary, infirmary

-tary: documen**tary**, secretary, hereditary, military, solitary, elementary

-lary: vocabu**lary**, salary, burglary,

-iary: diary, auxiliary

Plural spelling rule

When there's a consonant + y, change the "y" to "ies" (-**ary** to -**aries**)

anniversary — anniversaries	library — libraries
glossary — glossaries	dictionary — dictionaries
boundary — boundaries	summary — summaries
documentary — documentaries	burglary — burglaries
revolutionary — revolutionaries	secretary — secretaries
missionary — missionaries	primary — primaries
diary — diaries	

-ery Pattern

cemetery "ce-me-te-ry"
singular: cemetery Plural: *cemeteries*.
*A cemetery isn't **ee**rie with lots of g**ree**nery.*
statione**ry** = **e**nvelopes, pap**er**, p**e**ns, etc.

→ *very*, every, discovery, bravery, shivery, slavery, recovery
→ *battery*, mystery, artery, lottery, blustery, adultery, dysentery
monastery, flattery, watery, pottery
→ *robbery*, bribery, snobbery
→ *imagery*, surgery, forgery
→ *nursery*, misery → *grocery* → *cookery*, bakery
→ *confectionery, scenery, stationery, machinery, vinery*
→ *celery, cutlery, gallery* → *periphery* → *feathery, lathery, dithery*
→ *butchery, archery, treachery, lechery*

Notice how a lot of these words are formed:

cook — cooker — cookery	*bake — baker — bakery*
rob — robber — robbery	*brave — braver — bravery*
bribe — briber — bribery	*brew — brewer — brewery*
forge — forger — forgery	*recover — recovery*
image — imagery	*flatter — flattery*
slave — slavery	*stationer — stationery*
scene — scenery	*silver — silvery*
machine — machinery	*summer — summery*
nurse — nursery	*water — watery*
grocer — grocery	*feather — feathery*
pot — potter — pottery	*confection — confectioner — confectionery*

British vs. American
jewellery vs. *jewelry*

Plural spelling rule
When there's a consonant + **y**, change the **y** to **ies** (-**ery** to -**eries**)

cemetery — cemeteries	*discovery — discoveries*
battery — batteries	*mystery — mysteries*
forgery — forgeries	*discovery — discoveries*
brewery — breweries	*nursery — nurseries*
grocery — groceries	*surgery — surgeries*
bakery — bakeries	*robbery — robberies*

-ory Pattern

-tory: *lavatory, satisfactory, derogatory, promontory, inventory, laboratory, depository, inflammatory, directory, conservatory, mandatory, contradictory, explanatory, factory, territory, history, victory, predatory, dormitory, laboratory, exploratory*
-sory: *accessory, derisory, advisory, sensory, cursory, compulsory*
-gory: *category, allegory,*
memory, theory, ivory, story

Notice how some of these words are formed (-or to -ory)
contribut**or** — *contribut**ory***   invent**or** — *invent**ory***
director — *directory*   victor — *victory*
advisor — *advisory*   predator — *predatory*
sensor — *sensory*   auditor — *auditory*
supervisor — *supervisory*   respirator — *respiratory*

A lot of the words are linked to the **-tion** pattern:
satisfaction — *satisfactory*   preparation — *preparatory*
invention — *inventory*   exploration — *exploratory*
sensation — *sensory*   explanation — *explanatory*
direction — *directory*   circulation — *circulatory*
conservation — *conservatory*   inflammation — *inflammatory*

Plurals — change the **y** to **ies**
directory — *direct**ories***   memory — *mem**ories***
stories, theories, accessories, laboratories, victories...

Write an *-ory/-ories* story
This story is about a theory...

Word Families

Word families are linked by letter pattern and meaning. These visual links/patterns between words can help with spelling and help us understand why some words are spelt oddly.

> A **word family** is a group of words that have the same root and are related by meaning in some way.
>
> **vis** — **vis**ual, **vis**ion, **vis**ible, televi**s**ion
> **sign** — **sign**al, **sign**post, de**sign**, **sign**ature
> **oppose** — **oppos**ite, **oppos**ition
> **real** — **real**ly, **real**ise, **real**ity, un**real**, un**real**istic
> **know** — **know**ledge, **know**ing, **know**n/un**know**n, **know**s, ac**know**ledge

→ Some of the root words are not whole words but are letter patterns that make a word root. These were once part of a Latin root word, for example, **vis-** (*visual, vision, visible*) from Latin *visus* meaning 'sight.'

> These relationships in spelling help us to understand the meaning of words much more than the pronunciation does.
>
> Noam Chomsky

> The purpose of English spelling isn't about the sound but the visual links between words.
>
> Vivian Cook

> English spelling is often for the eye rather than the ear, and focussing on visual links can help us work out difficult words like homophones, silent letters and word order, like 'two' and 'light'.
>
> Johanna Stirling

> Although many times the spelling of a word may appear odd, an understanding of its origin can provide the most powerful key to remembering the spelling.
>
> Bear, Invernizzi, Templeton, Johnston: *Words Their Way.*

> → Noticing the word root can help your spelling, especially with tricky double or single letters. Look at these and decide which is correct.
>
> 1. vision or vission
> 2. disapear or disappear
> 3. teritory or territory
> 4. remember or remmember
> 5. memento or momento
> 6. mannual or manual

➔ Knowing the history and meaning of word roots can help your spelling. What do you think these Latin word roots/patterns mean?

1. **vis**: *visual, vision, visible...*
   -**vis**- means <u>to see/sight</u>

2. **appear**: *appear, disappear, appearance, reappear...*
   -**appear**- means _____

3. **terr**: *terrain, territory, subterranean...*
   -**terr**- means _____

4. **mem**: *memory, memo, memento, remember...*
   -**mem**- means _____

5. **man**: *manual, manufacture, manicure...*
   -**man**- means _____

6. **sign**: *signal, signpost, signature*
   -**sign**- means _____

7. **miss**: *transmission, submission, mission*
   -**miss**- means _____

8. **val**: *value, evaluate, valuation*
   -**val**- means _____

9. **rupt**: *rupture, erupt, bankrupt*
   -**rupt**- means _____

10. **mal**: *malfunction, malady, malpractice*
    -**mal**- means _____

Answers

1. **vis**: *visual, vision, visible...* **-vis-** means <u>to see/sight</u>

2. **appear**: *appear, disappear, appearance, reappear...*
   -appear- means <u>to come into view</u>

3. **terr**: *terrain, territory, subterranean...* **-terr-** means <u>earth</u>

4. **mem**: *memory, memo, memento, remember...*
   -mem- means <u>memory, mindful, remembering</u>

5. **man**: *manual, manufacture, manicure...* **-man-** means <u>hand</u>

6. **sign**: *signal, signpost, signature*
   -sign- means <u>to indicate, mark, a symbol</u>

7. **miss**: *transmission, submission, mission...* **-miss-** means <u>send</u>

8. **val**: *value, evaluate, valuation...* **-val-** means <u>worth or strength</u>

9. **rupt**: *rupture, erupt, bankrupt...* **-rupt-** means <u>to break/broken</u>

10. **mal**: *malfunction, malady, malpractice...* **-mal-** means <u>bad</u>

-vis- from Latin *visio(n-)* 'to see/sight'
vision, visual, visible/invisible, visibility, vista, visor,
revision, supervise, television, visit (go to see), *visitor*

-appear- from Latin *apparere* 'to come into view'
appear, appearance, appearing,
reappear, reappearance
disappear, disappearance

-terr- from Latin *terra* for 'earth, land, ground'
terrain, territory, terrace, subterranean, Mediterranean,
terracotta (earthen clay pot), *terra firma, terrestrial,*
extraterrestrial, terrier (a dog digging into the earth)

-mem- from Latin *memoria* for 'memory, mindful'
remember, memory, memorise/memorize, memorial,
memorandum, memo, memento, memorabilia, commemorate...

-man- from Latin for "hand"
manual (working with your hands) *manufacture,*
manicure, manipulate, manifesto, manuscript,
manacle, mandate, manage,
manoeuvre/maneuver (AmE)...

-sign- from Latin *signum* "to mark, indicate, a symbol"
sign, signpost, design, designer, redesign
signal, signature, signify, resignation...

Some of the words have a silent 'g' and others don't.
The voiced 'g' helps the pronunciation of the words: signature, signal, signify, resignation. Notice the "g" is voiced in a separate syllable, "sig":
"**sig**-nal", "**sig**-na-ture", "re-**sig**-na-tion".

-miss-/-mit- from Latin for "send"
trans**mit**/trans**miss**ion, submit/*submission,* omit/omission,
dismissal, permission, missile
mission, emission

-val- from Latin *valere* related to "worth or strength"
value, *evaluate, valuation, devalue, equivalent, interval...*

-rupt- from Latin for 'broken, to break'
rupture, inter**rupt**, *disrupt, disruption,*
erupt, eruption,
bankrupt, corrupt, abrupt...

-mal- from Latin for "bad"
malfunction, malpractice, malnourished, malady, malignant, malaria,
malcontent, malicious, malign, maladjusted, malevolent...

-ject-   -tract-   -struct-   -junct-   -spect-

1. Can you think of any words for these -ct- patterns?

2. a. Which of these patterns means **build**?
   b. Which of these means to **pull**?
   c. Which means to **throw**?
   d. Which means to **see/look**?
   e. Which means to **join**?

Some common words with the –ct- pattern

-**ject**– from Latin 'throw'
re*ject* (throw away!), re*jec*tion, e*ject*, pro*ject*ile, trajectory, pro*jec*tion (to throw light on something!), de*jec*tion, object, ob*jec*tion, trajectory, ad*ject*ive (to throw light on nouns!)...

-**struct**– from Latin for 'build'
structure, construction, constructive, instruct, instruction, destruct, destruction, reconstruction, obstruct...

-**spect**- from Latin for 'see/look'
inspect, inspector, inspection, spectator, spectacle, spectacles, aspect, spectacular, respect, circumspect, introspection, retrospective, speculate...

-**junct**– from Latin for 'join'
(Tricky pattern so remember the **j** and **n** in the meaning to **join**) junction, juncture, conjunction, injunction, adjunct, disjunction...

-**duct**-/-**duc**- from Latin for 'lead'
conductor, introduction, educate, induct, induction, viaduct, aqueduct, deduct, reproduce, reduce, duct, abduct...

-**sect**-/-**seg**- from Latin for 'cut'
section, sector, segment, intersect, bisect, dissect, insect...

-tract- from Latin for 'pull, draw out, or pull out'
tractor, extract, extraction,
retract, retractable, retraction,
attract, attraction, attractive, unattractive
contract, contractor, contractual
detract, distract, distraction, subcontract, subcontractor, subtract, subtraction...

Some Greek words roots

-graph- from Greek for 'write'
graph, graphics, paragraph, autograph, biograph, calligraphy

-path- from Greek for 'feeling, suffer'
sympathy, sympathetic, sympathise/sympathize, pathos
empathy (with feeling), *empathise/empathize,*
apathy (without feeling), *apathetic, antipathy, pathetic*

-phon- from Greek for 'sound'
phone, telephone, headphones, microphone, xylophone, symphony
photocopier, photosynthesis, photocell, photon
homophone, phonics, phoneme
cacophony (bad sound)

-photo- from Greek for 'light'
photograph (write with light), *photographer, photogenic, photocopier,*
photosynthesis, photon

-crit- from Greek for 'judge'
critic, criticise/criticize, critique, criterion, hypocrite

Exercise

What do you think these word roots mean?

1. **-man-** from Latin for '_____'
   manual, manufacture, manicure, manipulate, manifesto, manuscript, manacle, manoeuvre/maneuver(AmE), mandate, manage...

2. **-ped-** from Latin for '_____'
   pedicure, pedestrian, pedal, pedestal, expedition, moped, impede, expedite, orthopedic...

3. **-vis-** from Latin for '_____' *vision, visual, visible, visibility, vista, visor, visual, invisible, visitor, revision, supervise, television...*

4. **-aud-** from Latin for '_____'
   audio, audible, audition, auditorium, audience, inaudible, audiovisual

5. **-tang-/-tact-** from Latin for '_____'
   contact, tactile, tangible, intangible, tangent

6. **-dic-/-dict-** from Latin for '_____'
   dictate, diction, dictation, predict, dedicate, indict, predict, dictionary...

7. **-cogn-** from Latin for '_____'
   recognize/recognise, cognition, recognition, incognito, cognizant/cognisant

Answers

1. **-man-** from Latin for 'hand'
   manual (working with your hands) *manufacture, manicure, manipulate, manifesto, manuscript, manacle, mandate, manage, manoeuvre/maneuver* (AmE)...

2. **-ped-** from Latin for 'foot'
   pedicure, pedestrian, pedal, pedestal, expedition, moped, impede, expedite, orthopedic...

   Also, -**ped**- from Greek for 'child'
   pedagogy, pediatrician, paedophile (BrE)/*pedophile*

3. **-vis-** from Latin for 'seeing/vision'
   vision, visual, visible, visibility, vista, visor, visual, invisible, visitor, revision, supervise, television...

4. **-aud-** from Latin for 'hear'
   audio, audible, audition, auditorium, audience, inaudible, audiovisual

5. **-tang-/-tact-** from Latin for 'touch'
   contact, tactile, tangible, intangible, tangent

6. **-dic-/-dict-** from Latin for 'speak'
   dictate, diction, dictation, predict, dedicate, indict, predict, dictionary...

7. **-cogn-** from Latin for 'know'
   recognize/recognise, cognition, recognition, incognito, cognizant/cognisant

---

→ Next we're going to look at the numbers 'one' and 'two'

1. Why is there a "w" in **two**?

2. Why is there a "w" sound in **one**?

Two

Word families and visual links between words are very important to help us with spelling and understanding the meaning of words. They also help us understand why we have some "strange" patterns, like the 'tw' in *two* and the 'on' pattern in *one* and *once*.

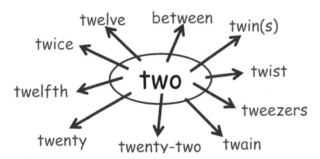

Notice the words in the diagram are all related to **two** in some way. *Twice*, *twelve* and *twenty* are obvious. There's also *twins* (two things alike), *between* (between two things), *tweezers* (two pieces of metal), *twist* (two things together), Twix (two chocolate biscuits). But the 'tw' is pronounced differently in *two*. Why?

In Old English/Anglo-Saxon, they had 'w' in the spelling *twā* and most likely pronounced it similar to the Dutch *twee*, and German *zwei*. Then it became silent, but remained in the spelling to show the history of the word.

One

one — once — only — none — alone — lonely are all related to *one* in some way. But *one* and *once* are pronounced differently.

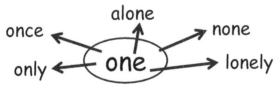

The 'w' sound was added to *one* and *once* in popular speech somewhere between 1150-1476, and became standard in the 17th century. We don't know why it happened. Pronunciation is always changing to make speaking/pronunciation easier, but the spelling remains fixed.

lone + ly = *lonely*
loneliness = lone + ly = *lonely* then change the 'y' to 'i' with ness = *loneliness*

alone is spelled as one word.

Exercise

Can you remember what these Latin stem words/patterns mean? Write in four words that belong to the pattern.

-val-

-ject-

-terr-

-man-

-tract-

-mal-

-vis-

➔ In the next chapter, we're looking at building words with prefixes and suffixes. Do you know what these are?

Look at this word: **uncomfortable**
Can you see the **root word, prefix,** and **suffix**?

These terms are so important to know because they help you spell, read, and understand words.

Building Words with Prefixes and Suffixes

Uncomfortably, disinterested, unmanageable, indifferently, unnecessarily, anticlockwise, misrepresentation...
Do long words scare you?

These complex words aren't so scary and difficult to learn if you know how they break down into manageable bits called *root words, prefixes,* and *suffixes*. Understanding how words are formed with linguistic building blocks is an important spelling strategy.

prefix + **root word** + suffix

uncomfortable

In the section on Spelling Systems, we saw how we can morph words with prefixes and suffixes (the *Morphological System*). This also involves spelling rules (The Graphemic System), and the history of spelling (The Etymological System).

prefix + **root word** + suffix

prefixes

The word **prefixes** itself morphs down into: **pre + fix + es.** The **-es** suffix is added to words ending in *x, z, s, sh, ch* to form plurals. More on suffix spelling rules later.

The *Oxford Dictionaries Online* says: Some prefixes and suffixes are part of our living language, in that people regularly use them to create new words for modern products, concepts or situations. For example:

security ➔ *biosecurity,* clutter ➔ *declutter,*
space ➔ *cyberspace,* media ➔ *multimedia,* email ➔ *emailer*

https://en.oxforddictionaries.com/spelling/prefixes-and-suffixes

Some new words from Merriam-Webster.com:
absorb ➔ *bioabsorbable,* binge ➔ *bingeable,* hacking ➔ *biohacking*

Maria Forleo's book: *Everything is Figureoutable*
figure out ➔ *figureoutable*

Prefixes are added straight onto the root word: *trust/mistrust, sure/unsure, patient/impatient*

Suffixes sometimes change the root word: *fit/fits/fitter/fitness, happy/happily/happiness*

We can create **word families** by adding prefixes and suffixes:

certain — *uncertain, certainty, certainly, uncertainly*

believe — *believable, unbelievable, believing, believed*

manage — *manager, manageress, managed, managing, manageable, unmanageable, management*

employ — *employed, employee, employer, employment, unemployed, employability*

know — *knowledge, knowledgeable, acknowledge, acknowledging, acknowledgement or acknowledgment, unacknowledged*

represent — *represents, represented, representing, representative, representatively, unrepresentative, representation, misrepresent, representations, misrepresenting, misrepresentation, representational*

You need to understand and to **see** that often the longest words are potentially the easiest to learn.

You need to understand that each part of the word carries meaning. In each word, there is a core element of meaning, which is the root of the word.

Sue Abell: *Helping Adults to Spell*

You can improve your spelling, increase your knowledge of words and spellings, and dramatically improve your confidence with spelling if you understand that long words are often made up of a "root" word plus "bits" added to the beginning and/or end (these "bits" are called prefixes and suffixes).

The Starter Pack, Basic Skills Agency

So knowing how words are built with prefixes and suffixes can help you spell complicated words and be less scared of them.

➔ Next, we're going to look at some common prefixes and rules.
   Add a prefix to these words to make the opposite meaning.

   1. ___correct   2. ___necessary   3. ___legal

   4 ___mature   5. ___appropriate   6. ___patient

Prefixes

> incorrect, unnecessary, illegal, immature, inappropriate, impatient,
> multinational, superstore, transatlantic, prearranged...

Prefixes are little words we add to the beginning of root words to make the word negative or add extra information.

There are hundreds of prefixes. Some of the most popular are:

in-, ir-, il-, im-, un-, dis-, pre-, ex-, anti-, uni-

The most common prefixes are **un-, re-, in-, dis-**

un + happy = **unhappy** = not happy = sad

un + comfortable = **uncomfortable** = not comfortable

un + usual = **unusual** = not usual, not common = odd, strange, extraordinary

re + paint = **repaint** = paint something again

re + do = redo = do something again

re + start = restart = start something again

in + correct = **incorrect** = wrong = not correct, not right

in + complete = **incomplete** = not complete, unfinished

in + appropriate = **inappropriate** = not appropriate, not useful, not suitable

dis + like = **dislike** = don't like

dis + integrate = **disintegrate** = destroy, separate into parts, break up

dis + satisfied = **dissatisfied** = not happy, not good, not as good

---

Notice how prefixes can enhance your vocabulary and give you a massive lexicon of words. Choose wisely, because adding some prefixes can make the word more formal or academic, and not appropriate for informal emails to family or friends! Look at the examples below.

*I am **dissatisfied** with the service I received on Saturday* (formal letter of complaint).
*I'm **unhappy** with the service I got on Saturday* (informal email to a friend).
*That's **wrong**! That's **incorrect**!*

➜Notice the double letters in the following words. We add the prefix to the root word and in doing so we get double letters:

di**ss**atisfied = dis + satisfied   mi**ss**pell = mis + spell

u**nn**ecessary = un + necessary   i**mm**ature = im + mature

i**rr**esponsible = ir + responsible   i**ll**egal = il + legal

ove**rr**ate = over + rate

Prefix Rules

Can you see the rules in these words?
illogical, illegal, illegible
irregular, irresponsible, irresistible
immature, immortal, immigrant
impossible, imperfect, impatient

There are plenty of exceptions to these rules, but the pronunciation can help. Historically, some prefixes were changed to aid speaking and pronunciation.

Prefix Rules and Exceptions

Use **il** before words starting with **l**
legible — *illegible, illegal, illuminate, illiterate, illogical*
illegally (so many l's) = il + legal + ly
(But also consider *unlawful, unlearn, unless...* 'un' helps the pronunciation)

Use **ir** before words starting with **r**
relevant — *irrelevant, irreconcilable, irregular, irradiate, irresistible*
irrelevantly = ir + relevant + ly
(But also consider *unreal, unrated...* 'un' helps the pronunciation)

Use **im** before words stating with **m, p, b**
mature — *immature, immigrant, immortal, immaculate,*
possible — *impossible*, perfect — *imperfect, impair, impact*
(But also consider *unpack, unpick, unpaid... unmarked, unmarried...*)

balance — *imbalance, imbecile, imbibe, imbue*
(But also consider *inbox, inbound, inbuilt...*)

Prefix Exercise

Make these into the opposite meaning by using a prefix:

1. sure _____

2. patient _____

3. able _____

4. certain _____

5. sense _____

6. legal _____

7. logical _____

8. responsible _____

9. shape _____

10. natural _____

11. spell _____

12. necessary _____

Answers

1. sure → unsure
2. patient → impatient
3. able → unable
4. certain → uncertain
5. sense → nonsense
6. legal → illegal
7. logical → illogical
8. responsible → irresponsible
9. shape → misshape
10. natural → unnatural
11. spell → misspell
12. necessary → unnecessary

Notes

Common prefixes with their meanings (some mean different things with different words).

un, in, il, im, ir, dis, non
These make nouns, verbs, adjectives into the negative, opposite meaning and mean "not".
unfair, untidy = not fair, not tidy
incomplete, informal, illegal, illegitimate,
immature, impatient, irregular, irrational,
dishonest, dislike,   non-smoker, non-toxic...

de, dis, un, re
These indicate reversal of a verb's actions - reverse, back, again.
defrost, debug, detach...
untie, unwrap, undo...
repaint, retry, redo, return, retell, regain...
disconnect, discontinue, disable...

over, under, sub, mis
These indicate something is wrong, bad, under, lowly or excessive.
oversleep (too much sleep), *overpopulated* (too many people, excessive)
undervalued (not valued enough), *undercooked* (not cooked enough)
substandard, subspecies, subservient...
misunderstand, miscalculate, misinterpreted, misinformed...

hyper, mega, super, ultra, micro, mini
These indicate size: very big, very small, too much.
hypermarket, hyperactive, hyperbolic...
megastore, megabyte, megabucks...
supermarket, supermodel, supertanker...
ultrasound, ultra-modern, ultraviolet...
microwave, microchip, microbrewery...
miniskirt, minibus, miniseries...

mono, uni, bi, tri, multi, semi
These indicate number, frequency, shape.
monorail, monologue = one
universal, unisex = one, or the same
bilingual, bicycle = two
triangle, tripod = three
semicircle, semicolon = half
multinational, multitasking = many

Hyphens (-) (Taken from my Punctuation Guide & Workbook)

> e-book or ebook, e-mail or email,
> Which is right?

Both are right. Hyphens come and go. When it's a new word, it usually starts with a hyphen so as not to confuse people, then soon the hyphen is dropped (*to-day* is now *today*, *e-mail* is now *email* but we can still use *e-mail*). This has been going on for centuries! Use a good dictionary to check the latest spellings with hyphens.

→You must use a hyphen when the prefix comes before a capital letter because a capital letter can't appear inside a word: *mid-July, anti-British, pro-European, anti-Semite, post-Vietnam, un-American, off-Broadway, ex-Foreign Secretary*

→Sometimes we add hyphens with prefixes, and sometimes not.

co-owner / coexist
pre-war / preview
anti-hero / antisocial
up-market / upbeat
off-site / offshore
non-negotiable / nonconformist

There are no rules about when to use a hyphen or when to write a prefixed word as one whole word. A good dictionary will help you.

→In American English they tend to drop the hyphen, and in British English they tend to keep the hyphen. It's all to do with clarity and understanding.

→Look at these words: *antiaging* vs. *anti-ageing*
antiaging is the American spelling
anti-ageing is British spelling
The British one with the hyphen (anti-ageing) is easier to read. But it depends on what you're used to seeing and reading.

→For single letter prefixes, most have hyphens.
X-ray, X-rated, X-certificate, U-turn, A-list, T-shirt, T-bone, Y-chromosome, T-junction/T-intersection... The single letter is a capital.

But these newer, internet-related words have lowercase single letters. The 'e' stands for *electronic: e-book/ebook, e-mail/email, e-commerce, e-bike, e-cash* (the hyphen will probably be dropped soon).

→If a word looks the same as another, we need the hyphen:
recover/re-cover — I have *recovered* from my illness.
I have *re-covered* my sofa.

remark/re-mark — She *remarked* that she needs to *re-mark* the test papers.

reform/re-form — The band is *re-forming* after breaking up ten years earlier and *reforming* its ways.

repress/re-press — I need to *re-press* my shirt.
I need to *repress* my memories.

→If you add a prefix to a word and it means there will be two vowels together with the same letter, we can split them with a hyphen: *re-enter, re-entry, re-election, co-own, anti-intellectual, pre-empt, pre-existing, co-op...* (otherwise, they can look confusing; reenter, coown, reelection, coop...). See the exceptions with 'co + o' below.

If there are two vowels together that can cause confusion, stick in a hyphen: *re-align (realign), de-ice (deice), co-author...*

But we also have: *The stamps have been reissued.* A hyphen after *re-* is not needed because there's no confusion with another word.

→With the prefix co-
co-op, co-opt, co-organizer, co-owner, co-chairman, co-host, co-pilot, co-star, co-worker, but not *coexist.*

In British English, we have *co-operate, co-operation, co-ordinate* or *cooperate* and *coordinate* without the hyphen.

In American English, there's no hyphen in: *cooperate, cooperation, cooperative, coordinate.*

→The prefix **self** usually has a hyphen when added to words:
self-doubt, self-conscious, self-esteem, self-righteous, self-belief, self-cleaning, self-assembly, self-adhesive, self-build, self-catering, self-censorship, self-centered, self-talk, self-taught, self-made, self-medicate, self-limiting, self-love, self-sacrifice, self-pity...

When we add a suffix to **self**, though, we don't add a hyphen: *selfless, selfness, selfhood, selfsame*

However, when adding *un* to *self-conscious*, we write *unselfconscious* (not *unself-conscious* x).

Suffixes

-s -y -ing -ment -ful -ly -ed -tion -ble...

prefix + **root word** + suffix
un**comfort**able
ir**regular**ly
mis**understand**ing
dis**respect**fully
misre**present**ations
(notice the 2 prefixes and 2 suffixes)

Suffixes, or common endings, are little words we put at the end of words to change the meaning and grammar.

Noticing suffix endings is so important because when English is spoken quickly, the ending sometimes sounds unstressed or disappears, or has the same sound as other suffixes.

Suffixes are extremely useful.

We can change the grammar:
walk — walks, walked, walking, walker
small — smaller, smallest, smallish
forgive — forgiving, forgiven, forgivable, forgiveness
smile — smiley, smiler, smiling, smiled, smilingly

We can make verbs:
simple — to simplify, simplified
sharp — to sharpen
real — to realize/realise
fright — to frighten

We can make job descriptions:
teach — teacher, electric - electrician, assist - assistant
act — actor, actress, waiter/waitress

We can make adjectives:
beauty — *beautiful*, fame — *famous*, self — *selfish*

A lot of **-ing** and **-ed** words are adjectives too: *frightening, scared, exhilarated, exhilarating...*

We can have more than one suffix ending:

hopefully = hope + ful + ly

presentationally = present + ation + al +ly

and more than one prefix and suffix together:

misrepresentations = mis + re + present + ation + s

If we take the root word, **employ**, and add other suffixes, we can make other words, such as **employed, employee, employer,** employment, employability...

We can add the **un** prefix to make the opposite meaning, **unemployed**, unemployment.

Both the spelling and the meanings of these words are linked. Remember, linked words like these are called a **word family**. We saw more in the section on Word Families.

Remember, we just add prefixes to the root word without changing anything, but with suffixes, we sometimes have to change the end letter, drop it, or double it.

For some spelling rules, we need to know vowel and consonant suffixes.

Some vowel suffixes are: **-ing, -ed, -er, -est, -ise/-ize, -or, -ary, -ery, -ur, -ent/-ence, -ant/-ance, -ous, -age, -ive, -ation**...

Some consonant suffixes are: **-s, -ly, -ness, -ment, ful, -cian, -tion, -sion, -less, -ward**...

Only Use Full when Full

Which is the correct spelling for these words?

hopeful or hopefull?

useful or usefull?

beautiful or beautifull?

➔ The suffix **-ful** is always spelt with one 'l'.

Answers
hopeful = hope + ful
useful = use + ful
beautiful = beauty, so change the 'y' to 'i' when adding a consonant suffix
beauti + ful

➔ By adding **-ful** to words, we can make adjectives or nouns:
wonderful, useful, successful, unsuccessful, dreadful, careful, helpful, unhelpful, hopeful, delightful, forgetful, frightful, thoughtful, peaceful, stressful, grateful, mindful, mouthful, cupful, armful, lawful, youthful, bagful...

➔ Careful: **grateful** is a common misspelled word. Don't spell it as greatful.
Grateful is from the obsolete word *grate* for "agreeable, pleasant," which is from Latin *gratus* meaning "pleasing".

➔ But when we add the suffix **-ly** to make adverbs or some adjectives, we then get **-fully (double 'l')**:
hope + ful + ly = *hopefully*, care + ful + ly = *carefully, usefully, successfully, beautifully, frightfully...*

➔ We usually keep the root word when adding **-ful**, but there are some British exceptions:
British English — American English
　　　skilful — skillful
　　　wilful — willful

➔ **Only use full when full**
Full up. Full marks. A full sandwich.
The train is full.

*If your **mind** is **full**, try **mindful** meditation to drop the load off.*

-ment

develop + ment = *development*   excite — *excitement*
commit + ment = *commitment*   achieve — *achievement*
govern + ment = *government*   endorse — *endorsement*
movement, equipment, improvement, harassment, embarrassment, assessment
merry — merriment (y to i)

According to the *Oxford Dictionary Online:* In British English, the normal spelling in general contexts is **judgement**. However, the spelling **judgment** is conventional in legal contexts, and in North American English.

-ness

-ness is from Anglo-Saxon and means state or quality, or condition.

➔ These are nouns formed from adjectives:

neatness — state of being neat
sadness — state of being sad
kindness, calmness, sweetness, bleakness, smoothness, wilderness, fitness
numbness, coolness, tenderness, madness, softness, goodness

➔ Don't drop the 'e' — *fierceness, blueness, hoarseness, awareness*

➔ Two suffixes — *helpfulness, blissfulness, mindfulness*

Notice the double 'n' in *meanness* (mean + ness), *drunkenness* (drunken + ness) =
suddenness, keenness, stubbornness, greenness, leanness, thinness

➔ Change **y** to **i**
happy — happiness, drowsy — drowsiness, lively — liveliness, weary — weariness, naughty — naughtiness, dizzy — dizziness, *lazy — laziness, ugliness, liveliness, clumsiness, loneliness, emptiness, tidiness*
cosy — cosiness (BrE)
cozy — coziness (AmE)

-less

➔ The suffix -**less** means without, not having, or free from:
colorless — without color
hopeless — not having hope
harmless, fearless, homeless, restless, ageless, faultless, soulless (soul + less)

➔ *y to i: penniless, pitiless, merciless*

➔ Combine **less** + **ness**
 harmlessness, fearlessness, homelessness, restlessness, agelessness, mindlessness, faultlessness

Syllable Breakdown

Syllable breakdown is a good strategy for spelling long words, and helps you remember the prefixes, suffixes and silent letters.

Breaking a word down into syllables means
- you break a word down into little spoken chunks,
- each chunk is called a syllable,
- each chunk usually has a vowel in it.

1 syllable: *trick*

2 syllables: *paper* — "pa-per"

3 syllables: *relevant* — "rel-e-vant" (4 syllables: "ir-rel-e-vant")

4 syllables: *difficulty* — "dif-fi-cul-ty"

5 syllables: *inappropriate* — "in-ap-pro-pri-ate"

6 syllables: *inappropriately* — "in-ap-pro-pri-ate-ly"

Breaking words down into syllables helps you spell a word if you say the syllables in a slow and exaggerated way — "Wed-nes-day". You can break words down however you want to — there is no right or wrong way. Break the word down the way that helps you.

> When you break a long word into syllables, you can tackle one small part at a time, and if you make a mistake, you can easily see which part of the word you need to work on.
>
> Basic Skills Agency: *The Starter Pack (1ˢᵗ ed)*

If you find it hard to identify syllables or hear them, no problem; see the words-within-words, the vowels, the root words, the prefixes and suffixes.

> Anne Betteridge says: "If breaking words into syllables doesn't make sense to you, then don't worry. Some people find it hard. A word can be broken up in several ways."
>
> **hearing**
> ⇨small words — h **ear** ing
> ⇨suffix endings — hear**ing**
> ⇨letter patterns — h**ear**, n**ear**, d**ear**, f**ear**
> ⇨say it oddly — "he" "a" "ring"
> ⇨memory trick — you h**ear** with your **ear** — hearing

Syllable breakdown	vs.	**Word breakdown** (words within words)
mis-un-der-stand-ing		mis-under-stand-ing
dis-con-nec-tion		dis-connect-ion
ex-am-i-na-tion		exam-i-nation
or ex-am-in-ation		

Breaking words into syllables also helps you remember the silent letter(s) in the word. Let's look at *Wednesday*.

Wednesday works well with syllable breakdown — it helps you remember the silent 'd' and 'e'.

We say "wens day," so when we break it down into **syllables** we have to say it slowly and exaggeratedly, incorporating all the letters:
"Wed" "nes" "day"

January and *February* can be broken down too, and will help you with the **-uary** pattern.
Say these slowly and exaggeratedly:
Jan-u-a-ry
Feb-ru-a-ry

Learn the letter pattern **-uary** "u/a/ry" for *Feb**uary*** and *Jan**uary***
and also ***br**r, it's Feb**r**uary!*

I use syllable breakdown for 2 words I have trouble with; *reluctant* and *hesitant*. I keep wanting to put an extra 'n' in *reluctant* and an extra 's' in hesitant!
re-luc-tant   hes-i-tant

Syllable breakdown helps with prefixes and suffixes:
hope-ful-ly   de-part-ment   un-friend-ly   im-ma-tur-i-ty
dis-ap-point-ed   un-will-ing-ness

Compound Words (toothpaste, football, snowman, breakfast)
Recognizing compound words is useful, especially when they have double letters or silent letters. If you break compound words down, this helps you spell them:
earring "ear ring," withhold "with hold," cupboard "cup board," hitchhiker "hitch hiker," bookkeeper, overrate, cupboard, handbag, breakfast, newspaper, etc.

Key Spelling Rules

People say spelling is chaotic — it's not. It's complicated, yes, but there are standards to it that can be learnt, and one way to do that is through learning spelling rules, which add another layer to your spelling knowledge.

Knowing spelling rules, and the exceptions to the rules, is a great strategy to help you understand why we spell words the way that we do.

Some people think if they learn a spelling rule, they'll be able to spell. Unfortunately, the trouble with rules is you have to remember the rule, and which words work with the rule and the words that don't! But some people like learning rules and get a buzz out of finding out how to use them.

So even if you forget the rule, maybe you'll remember the spelling pattern, and at least you hopefully will know why a spelling exists in the way it does.

A health warning: rules are complicated to explain, and there are many exceptions. "Good" spellers, who appear to understand spelling rules and principles, often apply other strategies. They may have good visual memories, which recognize differences in word construction. They may have learnt strategies (mnemonics or syllable counting) that have given them an understanding of how words behave, so they begin to "know" when spellings are wrong.

Basic Skills Agency: *Starter Pack*

This section is a brief look at five key rules. For an in-depth look at spelling rules, check out my *Spelling Rules Workbook — a step-by-step guide to the rules of English spelling*, available on my website and Amazon.

Preparation exercise

1. Why do we spell some words with -ly, -ely, -ally, or -lly?

2. Why do we keep the 'e' in *manageable* and *noticeable*, but drop the 'e' with other –able words like *believable* and *excitable*.

3. What's the difference between *hoping* and *hopping, taped* and *tapped, diner* and *dinner?*

4. Why do we double up the consonant in *referred, preferring* and *equipped* but not *referendum, preference* and *equipment?*

Read on and find out.

Top Five Spelling Rules

Rule 1. Adding -ly to words — 7 rules

1. Add -**ly** to whole words ending in a consonant:

slow + ly = *slowly*   quick + ly = *quickly*
anxious + ly = *anxiously*   care + less + ly = *carelessly*

2. Add -**ly** to words ending in l (this makes double l) ⟶

real + ly = *really*   total + ly = *totally*
usual + ly = *usually*   final + ly = *finally*

3. Add -**ly** to words ending in -**ful** (this makes double 'l' -fully) ⟶

careful + ly = *carefully*   hopeful + ly = *hopefully*
beautiful + ly = *beautifully*   faithful + ly = *faithfully,*

4. We usually keep the **e** (-ely):

love + ly = *lovely*   complete + ly = *completely*
immediate + ly = *immediately*   de + finite + ly = *definitely*

The big exception to this is often misspelled — *truly*
truly = true + ly ➔ drop the 'e' = *truly*
Also, due + ly = *duly*   whole + ly = *wholly*

5. Change the **e** to **y** in words ending in -ble, -tle, -ple...

simple ➔ *simply*   possible ➔ *possibly*
subtle ➔ *subtly*   probable ➔ *probably*

6. Change the end **y** to **i** in two syllable words ending in a consonant + y:

happy + ly = happily   crazy ➔ crazily   easy ➔ easily

But this doesn't apply to one syllable words: *shyly, slyly, coyly.*
But exceptions are: day ➔ *daily*   gay ➔ *gaily*

7. We add -**ally** to words ending in -ic: basic + ally = *basically*
ecstatic + ally = *ecstatically*
comically, cynically, ethically, logically, magically, medically, musically

⇨ A big exception is *publicly* = public + ly

If a word ends in -**al** just add ly (-**ally**): incidental ➔ *incidentally*
musical ➔ *musically, occasional* ➔ *occasionally*

Look at these patterns: *incident — incidental — incidentally*
occasion — occasional — occasionally   music — musical — musically
comic — comical — comically   magic — magical — magically

Rule 2. Drop the 'e' rule

➔ **Drop the 'e' with -ing**

come + ing = *coming*   write + ing = *writing*
complete + ing = *completing*   manage + ing = *managing*
argue + ing = *arguing*   congratulate + ing = *congratulating*
having, celebrating, changing, achieving, believing...

But not with words ending in -ee or -oe: *free — freeing, seeing, foreseeing, agreeing, guaranteeing, kneeing*
canoe — canoeing, hoeing, shoeing, tiptoeing

Or keep the 'e' if it changes the word to another meaning:
dye — dyeing (not dying), *singe — singeing* (not singing), *whingeing*

➔ **Drop the 'e' with –able/-ible**

achieve + able = *achievable*   believe + able = *believable*
response + ible = *responsible*   sense + ible = *sensible*
writable, arguable, believable, recognisable/recognizable,
collapsible, excusable, pleasurable...

We keep the 'e' with words ending in soft 'c' or 'g' to maintain the soft 'c' and 'g' sounds

notice + able = *noticeable*   manage + able = *manageable*
knowledge + able = *knowledgeable*   change + able = *changeable*
marriage + able = *marriageable*   service + able = *serviceable*

If the word has a hard "g" and "c" sound, we use –able: *navigable, delegable, despicable amicable, applicable, impeccable...*

Keep the 'e' with words ending in double 'e': *foreseeable/unforeseeable, agreeable*

➔ **Drop the 'e' with other vowel suffixes**
continue — *continuous, continued, continuator, continuing*
nerve — *nervous, nervy*
hesitate — *hesitant, hesitation, hesitating, hesitancy*
separate — *separation, separating, separable, inseparable*
adore — *adoration, adorable, adoring*
sense — *sensation, sensational, sensual*
prepare — *preparation, preparatory*

Careful, we drop the 'e' with a consonant suffix in these words:
argue — argument   awe — *awful* (but *awesome*)
   true —*truly*   whole — *wholly*   due — *duly*

Rule 3. Changing 'y' to 'i' rule

Happiness is a beautiful thing, but loneliness isn't.

If a two+ syllable word ends in a **consonant** + **y**, then **y** changes to 'i' when adding suffixes, but not with 'i' suffixes (-ing, -ish, -ible) because there will be two i's together *apliing, marriing*.

Change the 'y' to 'ies' for plurals and third person verbs.

tidy — *tidier, tidies, tidied, tidiest, tidily, tidiness*

beauty — beauti + ful = *beautiful, beauties, beautify, beautician*

happy — *happiness, happily, happier, happiest*

angry — *angrier, angriest, angrily*

ugly — *uglier, ugliest, ugliness*

busy — *busier, busiest, busily, business*

easy — *easier, easiest, easily*

crazy — *crazies, crazily, craziness, crazier, craziest*

lazy — *lazily, laziness, lazier, laziest*

lonely — *lonelier, loneliest, loneliness*

pretty — *prettier, prettiest, prettily*

reply — *replies, replied,* (**not** with -ing *replying ✓ repliing x*)

marry — *married, marriage, marries, marriageable* (**not** with -ing *marrying*)

apply — *applies, application, applied* (but *applying*)

empty — *emptied, empties, emptier, emptiest, emptiness* (not *emptying*)

study — *studied, studies, studious, studiously* (not *studying*)

necessary — *necessarily, unnecessarily*

temporary — *temporarily, temporariness*

ordinary — *ordinarily, ordinariness*

justify — *justified, justifies, justifiable, justification*

accessory — *accessories, accessorize/accessorise*

luxury — *luxuries, luxurious luxuriate, luxuriant, luxuriated*

Don't change for one syllable words: shy — *shyly,* sly — *slyly,* coy — *coyly,* wry — *wryly* (silent 'w')

But 'y' becomes 'i' in these -ay words:
day ➜ *daily*   gay ➜ *gaily, gaiety*
lay ➜ *laid, lain*   pay ➜ *paid*
say ➜ *said*

Rule 4. **1:1:1 doubling up rule** or the twinning rule

big - bigger, put - putting, biggest, quiz - quizzes

When a word has 1 syllable + 1 vowel next to 1 end consonant, we double up the final consonant with a <u>vowel suffix</u>:

sit — *sitter, sitting;* **big** — *bigger, biggest;* **tap** — *tapping, tapped*
hot — *hotter, hottest, hottie;* **sad** — *sadder, sadden, saddened, saddest*
blur — *blurring, blurred, blurry;* **shop** — *shopper, shopping, shopped*
fat — *fatten, fattening, fatter, fattest, fatty*
swim — *swimmer, swimming, swimmingly*
whiz — *whizzes, whizzed, whizzing, whizzer*
quiz — *quizzes, quizzed, quizzing, quizzer, quizzical*
('u' always follows 'q' in English words so 'u' is not classed as another vowel.)

Remember to only double up with vowel suffixes. Compare these:
*dropper/droplet, inner/inward, sunny/sunless
hottest/hotly, goddess/godly, shipping/shipment redden/redness,
swimmer/swims, strappy/strapless*

The 1:1:1 doubling up rule happens in longer words when the stress is on the final syllable:

begin "beGIN" — *beginner, beginning*
defer "deFER" — *defer, deferred, deferring* (not *deference*)
refer "reFER" — *referring, referred, referral*
(not *reference* "REFerence", *referendum*)
prefer — *preferred, preferring* (not *preferable, preference, preferential*)
occur "ocCUR" — *occurring, occurred, occurrence* "ocCURrence"
equip — *equipped, equipper, equipping* (but *equipment* - consonant suffix)
commit — *committed, committing, committable, committee*
forget — *forgetting, forgettable, forgotten*

➔We never double up *w, x, y* or *c*.

-c to -ck.
Words ending in -ic, we must add 'k' to keep the hard "c" sound:
picnic — *picnicking, picnicked, picnicker*
panic — *panicked, panicking, panicky*
traffic — *trafficking, trafficked*
mimic — *mimicking, mimicked* (but not *mimicry*)

Careful there are some double letters in compound words

Compound words are words that are made up of two words.

ear + ring = *earring*   book + keeper = *bookkeeper*

with + hold = *withhold*   room + mate = *roommate*

hitchhike, newsstand, barroom, knickknack...

Two exceptions are *wherever* and *pastime* = to pass time.

Rule 5. Adding -es to words

This is an easy rule. We add -es to present tense third person verbs (he, she, it) and plural endings with words ending in **s, ss, sh, ch, x, z.**

He watches lots of football matches while she watches quizzes and relaxes with boxes of chocolates.

We put **–es** on the end of these words because it separates the 's' from the other s's and z's (gass, passs, quizzs x)

gas — *gases, bus — buses*

pass — *passes, glass — glasses, waitress — waitresses*

confess — confesses, business — businesses

dish — *dishes, wash — washes, wish — wishes*

match — *matches, watch — watches, catch — catches*

rich — riches, church — churches, beach — beaches

box — *boxes, fox — foxes, relax — relaxes*

quiz — *quizzes, whiz — whizzes, fizz — fizzes*

Exception: if the **-ch** ending is pronounced with a "k" sound, you add **–s**: stomach — *stomachs*, epoch — *epochs*.

A couple of useful little rules to know

In British English, we drop the 'u' in –our words with –ary, -ous, -ist, -ise/-ize, making it the same as the American spelling.

British — British and **American**

honour — *hon<u>o</u>rary*

labour — *laborious*

humour — *humorous, humorist*

amour — *amorous*

rigour — *rigorous, rigorist*

vigour — *vigorous*

glamour — *glamorous, glamorise/glamorize*

Drop 'u' in the -ous when adding –sity
(the pronunciation helps, and also breaks into syllables well)
generous — *generosity*   curious — *curiosity*   virtuous — *virtuosity*
monstrous — *monstrosity* fabulous — *fabulosity*   pompous — *pomposity*

Change the **-cious** to **-city**
(notice the sound changes from "sh" to "s")
fero**cious** — *ferocity*
atrocious — *atrocity*
precocious — *precocity*
pugnacious — *pugnacity*

An understanding of spelling rules helps you discover more rules and riddles for yourself. This fuels interest, engagement and thinking skills.
Sally Raymond: *Spelling Rules, Riddles and Remedies*

Exercise. Use your knowledge of these spelling rules, or visual memory, to decide which is correct.

1. a. mooddy b. moody

2. a. bloodiest b. bloodyest

3. a. fraudulent b. frauddulent

4. a. foxxy b. foxy

5. a. boxes b. boxs

6. a. reference b. referrence

7. a. iffy b. ify

8. a. truly b. truely

9. a. panicing b. panicking

10. a. watchs b. watches

> *An understanding of spelling rules gives you another lens through which to view spelling.*
>
> Sally Raymond: *Spelling Rules, Riddles and Remedies*

Answers

1. a. mooddy   **b. moody**

2. **a. bloodiest**   b. bloodyest

3. **a. fraudulent**   b. frauddulent

4. a. foxxy   **b. foxy**

5. **a. boxes**   b. boxs

6. **a. reference**   b. referrence

7. **a. iffy**   b. ify

8. **a. truly**   b. truely

9. a. panicing   **b. panicking**

10. a. watchs   **b. watches**

12. a. forgoten   **b. forgotten**

Spelling Rules and Suffixes Revision Exercise

word	root word	suffix(es)	spelling rule(s)
happiness	happy	ness	change y to i
wishes			
beginning			
slowly			
generosity			
forgotten			
busiest			
responsible			
finally			
picnicking			
changeable			
arguing			
hopefully			
beautician			

Answers

word	root word	suffix(es)	spelling rule(s)
happiness	happy	ness	change **y** to **i**
wishes	wish	es	add **es** to **sh**
beginning	begin	ing	doubling up rule
slowly	slow	ly	add **ly**
generosity	generous	-ity /-sity	drop the **u**
forgotten	forgot	en	doubling up rule
busiest	busy	est	change **y** to **i**
responsible	response	-ible	drop the **e**
finally	final	ly	add **ly**
picnicking	picnic	ing	add **k** to **c**
changeable	change	able	keep the **e** to keep the soft **g** sound
arguing	argue	ing	drop the **e**
hopefully	hope	ful + ly	add **ful** + **ly**

Suffixes Affecting Pronunciation

Adding a suffix to some root words can change the pronunciation of the vowel sound, or make a silent letter voiced, for example:

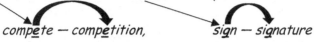

compete — competition,   sign — signature

> "Words that are related in meaning are often related in spelling as well, despite changes in sound." Chomsky
>
> This in turn supports a powerful spelling strategy, according to the authors of *Words Their Way*. If you are unsure how to spell a word, try to think of a word that is similar in meaning and structure to one that you *do* know how to spell.

Long to *short* vowel sound

If you drop the 'e' and add a suffix, it changes the vowel sound to a short sound. which is voiced in a separate syllable. "com-pet-it-tion", "san-i-ty"

(Remember the vowel closest to the end 'e' — the magic 'e'/silent 'e' — is usually long.)

Long — Short

compete — *competition*
define — *definition*
ignite — *ignition*
invite — *invitation*
adore — *adoration*
reside — *resident*
sane — *sanity*
divine — *divinity*
serene — *serenity*
obscene — *obscenity*
extreme — *extremity*
grave — *gravity*

long vowel/soft 'c' — short vowel/hard 'c'
introduce — *introduction*
produce — *production*
reduce — *reduction*

Notice the short vowel sound is voiced in a separate syllable:
"com-pet-it-tion", "san-i-ty", "in-tro-duc-tion"

Sometimes a letter can be silent in one word but not in others. This usually occurs when a suffix has been added.

silent — *voiced*
sign — *signal, signature*
resign — *resignation*
condemn — *condemnation*
crumb — *crumble, crumbling*
bomb — *bombard*
muscle — *muscular*
solemn — *solemnity*
debt — *debit*
limb — *limber*

These silent letters are kept in words to help to connect different forms of the same word. The silent letters are voiced to make the pronunciation easier.

But some silent letters still remain in some words:
climb — climber — climbing — climbed

The "g" in the **sign** word family can be silent or voiced:
silent: *sign, signage, signpost, design, designer, redesign*
voiced: *signal, signature, signify, resignation, designated*

Notice the "g" is voiced in a separate syllable "sig":
"**sig**-nal", "**sig**-na-ture", "re-**sig**-na-tion"

"de-**sig**-na-ted" ("zig" sound)

To sum up this section on prefixes and suffixes, a few words from Darren Johnson. Read his story in *the Your Stories* section.

You start to see that you only need to add a few letters and you have a new word, and you start to learn that you don't need to learn an 8 or 9 letter word, you just need to add a few letters to the 4 or 6 letter word you have learnt.

Exercise

Take away the suffix to find the root word. Don't forget your spelling rules, or if a letter was dropped, or doubled up, or changed!

biggest — <u>big</u>

friendship _____

quietly _____

sadness _____

hoping _____

secondary _____

employment _____

funnily _____

confusing _____

magician _____

beginner _____

professional _____

imaginary _____

happiness _____

beautiful _____

simplify _____

quizzes _____

decision _____

Answers

biggest — big

friendship — friend

quietly — quiet

sadness — sad

hoping — hope

secondary — second

employment — employ

funnily — funny

confusing — confuse

magician — magic

beginner — begin

professional — profession

imaginary — imagine

happiness — happy

beautiful — beauty

simplify — simple

quizzes — quiz

decision — decide

Exercise

Break these words into their prefix, suffix and root word.

	prefix	root word	suffix
e.g. international	inter	nation	al
unthinkable			
misunderstanding			
illegally			
disappointed			
transformed			
unbelievable			
impatiently			
unwillingness			
unfriendly			
multinational			
resignation			
irresistible			

Answers

Break these words into their prefix, suffix and root word.

	prefix	root word	suffix
international	inter	nation	al
unthinkable	un	think	able
misunderstanding	mis	understand	ing
illegally	il	legal	ly
disappointed	dis	appoint	ed
transformed	trans	form	ed
unbelievable	un	believe	able
impatiently	im	patient	ly
unwillingness	un	willing	ness
unfriendly	un	friend	ly
multinational	multi	nation	al
resignation	re	sign	ation
irresistible	ir	resist	ible

Phonic Spelling Strategies

Patterns, Rhymes, Sounds and Rules

Even though English is only about 50% phonetically regular, good spellers always try to sound out a word if they're not sure of the spelling because sound is the first element of a word we have reference for, and certain patterns go with certain sounds. Good spellers they try to hear if it sounds like a word or pattern they know how to spell, and then when they write it, they use their visual memory and knowledge of rules and patterns to see if it's right.

Listening to sounds can help you spell but it's an unreliable strategy which needs backing up with other strategies.

An understanding of phonics can help with the spelling of **regular** words. You might not have come across a word before but, if it is regular, then you stand a good chance of being able to work it out. For instance, you might never have seen the word "chitterling", but you can read it (and possibly even be able to spell it) because you will recognize bits of the word: **ch** as in **ch**urch, **itter** as in l**itter**, **ling** as in fal**ling**

Anne Betteridge: *Adult Learners' Guide to Spelling*

We have 26 letters in the English alphabet and over 44 different sounds (and more with our many English accents). Some letters have to do more than one job, and we also have to combine letters.

We have single consonants, and consonant blends:
beginning: br-, bl-, sc-, st-, sw-, gl-, pr-, spr-, str-, thr-, shr-
end: -st, -sp, -sk, -pt, -lf, -lp, -nk, -ng, -nt, -ck, -tch, -dge

We can use rhyming to help:
flag, brag, drag, shag, snag, blag, stag
-ink, pink, sink, wink, drink, stink, think
-ing, ping, sing, wing, ring, sting, thing

There are 20 standard vowel sounds (and many more because of accents). But we only have 5 vowel letters (a, e, i, o, u) with the occasional addition 'y' depending on its position within a word. To create all of the vowel sounds we use, we combine vowels: -ee-, -ea-, -ie-, -ei-, -uo-, -ui-, -oi-, -ow-, -oy-.

But these vowel patterns can have different sounds. They can be long, short or a diphthong (2 vowel sounds in one syllable — *coin, side, loud*), so developing your visual memory, knowledge of rules, and patterns is important.

> Every word, and every syllable within a word, must have a vowel sound, otherwise, we would not be able to say or hear words clearly at all.
>
> Lyn Stone: *Spelling for Life*

Building your spelling knowledge of letter patterns and their sounds, understanding long and short vowel sounds and how they can be influenced by single and double consonants, and seeing spelling rule patterns, can all help with your spelling.

What are long and short vowel sounds?

Let's look at these without going too "linguistic" and academic! Don't worry if you don't know these, or can't hear them. I wasn't taught them at school. I bet you weren't either, which is a shame because they can influence and help spelling and reading.

Long vowel sounds: *dream, need, soon, please, rain.* They can also have a single vowel: *phone, kind, say.* They are spoken the same way as their alphabet name "a, e, i, o, u" = "ay", "ee", "eye", "oh" "you". We also combine these to make diphthongs: -oi-, -oy-, -ow-, -ai-.

Notice how the spelling of the sounds can vary:
e — "ee" *please, dream, key/quay, these, thief, evening, equal*
i — "eye" *kind, buy/bye, pint, dive, light, high, guide*
o — "oh" *phone, bold, toe/tow, ozone, broke, flown, old*
a — "ay" *say, tail/tale, break, page, alien, racing, eight*
u — "you" *use, cute, super, tuna, fruit, new, who*
y — "eye" *cry, why, shy, supply, try*

Be careful of these homophones. These words sound the same but have different meanings and spellings of the long vowel sound:
steak/stake, break/brake, aisle/I'll/isle, ate/eight, be/bee, bean/been, blew/blue, brews/bruise, buy/by/bye, ceiling/sealing, cereal/serial, chews/choose, cue/queue...

Consonants can also make a vowel long, for example,
-gh- makes the 'i' long in *sigh, sight, high, light, flight*
-nd makes the 'i' long in *wind* (a clock), *kind, mind, find, grind*
-w *saw, law, flaw, new, chew, blew, stew, few, blow, grown, know, snow, low...*
r-influenced: *car, star, dark, scare, near, year, herb, herd, third, shirt, bird, skirt, girl, curd*
l-influenced: *walk, talk, folk, yolk, fold, told, sold, cold, roll*

Short vowels: a in <u>a</u>pple, e in <u>e</u>gg, i in <u>i</u>nch, o in <u>o</u>dd, u in <u>u</u>nder

Short vowel sounds are usually simple to spell. But there are a few traps.

red but *dead*	*bed* but *head*
mist but *mystery*	*Jim* but *gym*
on but *swan*	*rod* but *squad*
nutty but *nothing*	*bubble* but *trouble*

Shireen Shuster: *Spelling Essentials*

We're going to look at some interesting consonant patterns and how we use them with short and long vowel sounds.

Long and short vowel sound comparison

short	ban	Ben	bin	bonny	bun
long	bane	bean/ been	bind	boney	
short	bat	bet	bit	bot	but
long	bait	beat/ beet	bite	bowtie	beauty
short	scratch	stretch	stitch	Scotch	such
long	scrape	streak	stride	scooch	surge
short	pat	pet	pit	pot	put
long	pate	Pete/ peat	pint	poetry	putrid
short	pack	peck	pick	pock	puck
long	park	peak/ peek	pike	poke	puke
short	gnat	net	knit	not/ knot	nut
long	nature	neat	night	note	newt
short	can	Ken	kin	con	come
long	cane	keen	kind	cone	coma
short	had	head	hid	hod	hud/hood
long	shade	heed	hide	hole	who

Some spelling rules
magic 'e' silent 'e'
Read the words below and hear the differences:

short vowel sounds / long vowel sounds
hop / *hope*
cut / *cute*
slim / *slime*
not / *note*

When we put a silent 'e' at the end of words, we make a new word with a long vowel sound. This silent 'e' at the end of words, following a single vowel and a consonant, usually makes the vowel long (but we have some exceptions with common function words: *come, have, some, done, love, glove*).

When we drop the 'e' with vowel suffixes, the long vowel sound is kept:

hope — hoping
tape — taping
use — usage
manage — manager
write — writable
believe — believable
note — notable
hate — hatred

The silent 'e' doesn't have to come at the end of a word: *Peter, baker, driver, winery, hopefully, used...*

Some common exceptions: *ever, never, clever, seven, eleven*

Some long vowel sound patterns

tale/tail	teem/team	tile	toe/tow	true
day	dean	dine	doe	do
cake	key/quay	kind	co	coupon
bait/bate	beat/beet	buy/bye	bold	beauty
page	please	pint	phone	blue

Patterns with -ol- usually indicate a long vowel sound. -O- says its alphabet name "oh", which is a long vowel sound.

old, bold, cold, fold, old, hold, mold, sold, told, wold, scold, soldier,
bolt, colt, dolt, holt, jolt, volt
folk, yolk
boll, droll, poll, scroll, toll

-oast
boast, coast toast, roast

-ost
host, ghost, post, most

-aste
taste, waste, baste, paste, chaste, chasten

-ange
change, danger, range, strange, exchange, arrange, grange, angel

-ind
find, bind, kind, rind, mind, behind, blind

-igh
high, sigh, light, night, fight, fright, sight, right, bright, blight, flight, plight, tight, knight, might, uptight, tonight, alright...

-ite
bite, site, write, white, polite, quite, unite, excite, kite...

Write letter pattern sentences or stories to practise/practice (AmE) these.
I was quite polite not to shout at the crazy kite flyer.
Let's toast a coast to boast about.

Short Vowel Sounds

One little letter can alter the meaning and sound of words.

sit	set	sat	slot	shut
pit	pet	pat	pot	put
mitt	met	mat	mot	mutt
hill	hell	Hal	hold	hull/Hull
pick	peck	pack	pock	puck
kin	Ken	can	con	come
bid	bed	bad	bod	bud
Sid	said	sad	sod	sudden
hid	head	had	hod	hud/hood
bitch	etch	batch	botch	butch
bib	--	babble	bobble	bubble
bitter	better	batter	blotter	butter
bigger	beggar	bagger	blogger	bugger

Flossy words

One syllable words ending in **F, L** or **S** (FLOSSY) double these letters after a short vowel:

pull, hull, full, dull, bull, bill, hill, pill, will, kill, till, ill, still, fill,
bell, hell, sell, cell, well, tell, fell, yell, smell, shell, spell...   shall, drill
(Exceptions: long sound in *all, ball, call, tall, fall, wall, small, stall*)

off, staff, Jeff, cuff, gruff, buff, fluff, huff, muff, puff, stuff, scruff,
cliff, toff, naff
kiss, hiss, piss, miss, bliss, Swiss, cross, toss, loss, floss, fuss, mess, less,
guess, dress, lass, mass,
painless, harmless, homeless, darkness, illness, kindness
express, impress, process, depress, success, discuss
pass, glass, grass (These are a long "ar" sound "glarss" in some accents.)

Exceptions: *of, if, us, pal, gas, bus, yes, chef, clef, plus*

Double consonants

Usually, one vowel followed by two consonants in words of more than one syllable indicates it's a short vowel sound:

dad — daddy, gran — granny, mum — mummy, rabbit, sorry, silly, letter,
supper, dinner, poppy, difficult, chubby, rubbish, follow...

But there are lots of exceptions: *melon, salad, cabin, treble, habit, body...*

Spelling rule
hop — hopping, hopper
sit — sitting, sitter
swim — swimming, swimmer
stop — stopping, stopped, stopper, stoppable
slop — sloppy
big — bigger, biggest, biggish

swimming

This is the 1:1:1 doubling up rule = 1 syllable: 1 vowel: next to 1 end consonant (see Spelling Rules section for more on this rule).

Exceptions: We never double up **c** or **k** in English words, but use -**ck** to indicate a short vowel sound: *check, chick, chock, chuck, chicken, wreck, Rick, rack, rock, ruck, racket, jacket, chocking, rocked...*

We never double up the letter **x** or **v** except in *revving, revved.*

→ Read these pairs, and notice the short vowel sound has two consonants.
long / short
super / supper
diner / dinner
coma / comma
later / latter
striped / stripped
slimiest / slimmest
hoping / hopping
taping / tapping
biter / bitter
lose / loss

→ Remember, double consonants usually mark a short vowel sound. Knowing this not only helps your spelling but your reading too.
*I was **hopping** mad and was **hoping** he wasn't home.*
*Let's go to the **diner** and have **dinner**.*
*That's a **super** idea for **supper**.*

→ What do you notice about these words? Read them aloud.
itch — each
pitch — peach
bitch — beach
tetchy — teach

-tch vs. –ch

> *itch — each*
> *pitch — peach*
> *bitch — beach*

The **-tch** ending indicates a short vowel sound, and follows a one-letter vowel.

-atch	-etch	-itch	-utch	-otch
snatch	stretch	stitch	-	Scotch
catch	ketchup	kitchen	clutch	crotch
batch	etch	bitch	butch	botch
patch dispatch	wretch sketch	witch twitch	crutch	blotch watch* (*pronounced "wotch")

Homophone*: which — witch*
Which witch is which?

We have some exceptions with common words ending in -ch: *rich, enrich, such, much, which, touch, attach, sandwich, ostrich, spinach, duchess, detach, bachelor, attach, detach.*

-**ch** is exactly the same sound as –**tch**. The 't' doesn't affect the sound of "ch". Read them aloud and see — *which/witch, itch/each, butch/such, pitch/peach...*

The *Oxford Dictionary* says these words often cause problems. A common mistake is to spell *attach* and *detach* with –tch.

If the final "ch" sound comes after a consonant, the ending is –*ch: inch, search, church, branch, pinch, winch.*

If the final "ch" comes after a two-letter vowel, the ending is –ch: *each, beach/beech, teach, reach, speech, touch, crouch.*

https://www.lexico.com/en/grammar/words-ending-in-ch-and-tch

Spelling rule

We add **es** to **ch** to make plurals and third person 's' (he, she, it).

watch — watch**es**   match — matches   blotch — blotches
peach — peaches   rich — riches   witch — witches
snatch — snatches   catch — catches   sketch — sketches

Compare these short vowel sounds to the long ones.

rich — reach
bitch — beach
pitch — peach

Careful with the spelling. There are probably more problems with speaking these, especially for people with English as a second language:
To reach the beach. vs. *To rich the bitch.*
The pitch is on the bitch. vs. *The pitch is on the beach.*

Use rhyming to help spell when you know one of these spellings.
match, snatch, catch, batch...
Careful, *watch* is pronounced *"wotch"*.
Dutch, hutch, butch, but also *such, much, touch*
fetch, stretch, etch, sketch
rich, bitch, stitch, witch, itch

Long vowel sounds
each, peach, beach/beech, reach, teach, speech

Write a –tch and –ch letter pattern story or a sentence.

-dge vs. **-ge**

Say the following and notice the short and long vowel sounds and patterns

short vowel sound vs. long vowel sound

cadge — cage
ridge — rage
Madge — page
edge — age
sludge — deluge
fudge — huge

English words don't end in **j**, we use **-dge** or **-ge**.

Notice **judge** has a "j" sound at the beginning and end.

-dge = short vowel sound:
badge, Madge, cadge, badger
edge, hedge, ledge, wedge, pledge, ledger, sledge
Exceptions: Abbreviations: *veg, reg*
ridge, bridge, fridge, porridge, midge
dodge, lodge, lodger, stodge
judge, budge, fudge, nudge, grudge, smudge, sludge, misjudge
dodgy, podgy, pudgy

No 'd' if there's another consonant:
plunge, bulge, gunge, orange, sponge, hinge, dungeon

Use **-age** or **-ege** when the word is more than one syllable: *village, garage, cottage, collage, garbage, damage, bandage, marriage, pillage, spillage, college, allege*

Long vowel sounds

-ge = a long sound in: **age**, *page, sage, stage, cage, huge, luge, deluge, rage, cage, wage, refuge, rampage, collage*

-ange
Long "a" sound with **-nge**: *range, change, grange, strange, danger, angel*

-rge
r-influenced long sound with **-rge**: *charge, large, Marge, barge, forge, surge, merge, gorgeous, George, splurge*

-ck, -ke, -k

→ Why do we have *-k, -ke, -ck* when they sound the same?

Jack and **Jake** make **pancakes** and **bake cakes** all **week**, and then **like** playing **hockey** and **whacking** a ball at **weekends**.

Long vs. Short Vowel Sounds

short — long
Mick — Mike
Jack — Jake
luck — Luke
lick — like
back — bake
cock — coke
whack — wake
sack — sake
shack — shake
black — Blake
block — bloke
quack — quake*

→ Notice the words in both columns have **one vowel** before the **-ck** and **-ke**. But the **-ke** ending has a long vowel sound because of the magic 'e' silent 'e' at the end: *cake, take, bake, coke, provoke, bloke, spoke, mistake, pancake, awake, like, bike, pike, hitchhike...*

*Normally, there's just one vowel before the –ck, but in *quick* and *quack* you can see two vowels together. In English words, Q always comes with U, so it's classed as one consonant -qu-.

quack, quick, quacking, quickly = short vowel sounds

We drop the 'e' with -ing and still maintain the long sound: *liking, baking, making, provoking...*

⇨ Remember, we don't double up the **k** or **c** to indicate a **short vowel** sound but use the **-ck** ending:

Mick, lick, pick, knick, flick, kick, chick, gimmick, carsick
whack, sack, back, tack, jack, knack, flack, black, attack, ransack
luck, duck, suck, tuck, truck, potluck
dock, lock, rock, sock, clock, block, hammock, padlock
neck, peck, deck, speck, fleck

-**ck**- can be found in the middle of words: *jacket, whacking, pocket, blockage, crackers, pucker, docket, socket, chicken...*

Double k happens in some foreign borrowed words: *trek — trekking, trekked*

Mick vs. *Mike*
Mick = a short sound because of -ck
Mike = a long sound because of the magic 'e' silent 'e'

-k
two vowels + k = a long sound
leak, peak/peek, beak, teak
cheek, seek, meek, cheek, reek, week/weak
break, steak, soak, sleek, croak, geek, streak

Exceptions: *book, cook, look, nook, hook, took, rook, shook, brook...* These used to be pronounced with a long "oo" sound, and in some accents, they still are.

'r' influenced long sound: *dark, bark, park, snarky, lark, mark, shark perk, Dirk, Turk, lurk,*

'l' influenced long sound:
"ork" — walk, talk, chalk, stalk
"oak" — folk, yolk

-nk = short sound:
ink, think, blink, wink
thank, Hank, bank
sunk, dunk, funk, chunk, skunk, slunk, trunk, junk, bunk

Long to short vowel sound change

Some root words change their vowel sound when we add suffixes. This happened during the Great Vowel Shift from 1300 when many vowel sounds changed or disappeared.

Notice how the vowel sound changes, and how hard it would be to say the words in the second column if there wasn't a sound change!

long — short
five — fifth/fifty/fifteen
south — southern
type — typical
hero — heroine
heal — health/healthy
decide — decision
grateful — gratitude
shade — shadow
clean — cleanliness
female — feminine
define — definite, definitive
divine — divinity
mime — mimic
holy — holiday
crime — criminal
please — pleasant, pleasure
mean — meant

Drop the i

Look at these words and notice how we drop the 'i' in the -ai- pattern when adding certain vowel endings. Notice the sound change.

long — short
explain — explanation, explanatory
Spain — Spaniard, Spanish
exclaim — exclamation
proclaim — proclamation
reclaim — reclamation
acclaim — acclamation
prevail — prevalent, prevalence

-ai- to -e-

We also replace the -ai- with -e- in the following words (notice the long to short sound change):

*maintain — maint**e**nance*

(Although *maintenance* often implies the *maintaining* of something, the word does not have *maintain* in it)

*detain — det**e**ntion*
retain — retention
attain — attention
sustain — sustenance
abstain — abstention
despair — desperate

-ei- to -e-

We have long to short in:

*rece**i**ve — reception*
*dece**i**ve — deception*
*conce**i**ve — conception*
*perce**i**ve — perception*

Look at *pronounce* and *pronunciation*. Notice the spelling of *pronunciation* — the 'o' is dropped.

Before writing the word out, say both *pronunciation* and *pronounce* out loud, and hear the difference.

We can use syllable breakdown for *pronunciation* — "pro-**nun**-ci-a-tion".

*A **nun** likes **pro**per **pro**nunciation but doesn't like to pronounce it **lou**dly.*

See words-within-words for *pronounce* – an **ounce** of pron**ounce**.
Or use rhyming and sentences: *ounce, announce, bounce, pounce.*
I want to announce how to pronounce an ounce of bounce.
When you announce it, please don't mispronounce an ounce of it.

Next, we're going to look at the rules around **-le words**.

➔Read the following pairs of words aloud. Look at them. What do you notice?

idle / middle
maple / apple
Google / goggle
gable / gabble

-le words

Did you notice how the single and double consonants change the vowel sound?

long vowel sound / short vowel sound

idle / middle
maple / apple
Google / goggle
gable / gabble

➡ Did you notice the words in the first column have long vowel sounds and one consonant before -le: *idle, maple, Google, gable?*

⇨ The second column words have short vowel sounds, and so have double letters: *middle, apple, goggle, gabble.*

idle and **middle**
➡ *idle* has a long vowel sound so -**dle**
⇨ *middle* has a short vowel sound so -**ddle**

maple and **apple**
➡ *maple* has a long vowel sound so -**ple**
⇨ *apple* has a short vowel sound so -**pple**

➡ *able, cable, table, fable, gable, sable, stable, enable*
⇨ *babble, dabble, drabble, gabble, grabble, rabble, scrabble*

➡ *noble, ennoble, Grenoble, ignoble*
⇨ *nobble, bobble, cobble, gobble, hobble, nobble, knobble, wobble*

➡ *idle, sidle, bridle*
⇨ *middle, diddle fiddle, piddle, riddle, griddle, twiddle*

The spelling/English guru, David Crystal, says something interesting about these short vowel -le words, and how most of them express a sound that reflects real life. They have onomatopoeic qualities (they sound like the sound that they refer to).

⇨ Read them aloud and see what he means: *bubble, babble, dabble, crumble, dribble, dazzle, nibble, rubble, wobble, rabble, chuckle, speckle, twinkle, trickle, wriggle, squiggle, wiggle, fiddle, twiddle, piddle, diddle, shuffle, sniffle, snuffle, snuggle, gabble, gobble, giggle, wobble, topple, rustle, haggle, cuddle, huddle, dapple, frazzled, sizzle, drizzle, guzzle, grizzle*

Of course, like anything about spelling, there are plenty of exceptions.

David Crystal: *Words, Words, Words*

Now write some fun sentences with these -le words.

Exercises

1. Change **a** to **o** in the following words:

cat <u>cot</u>   paint _____   broad _____

farmer _____   grain _____   boat _____

ward _____   fail _____   shave _____

care _____   bath _____   glass _____

2. Change the **i** to **e**:

pin <u>pen</u>   miss _____   flick _____

pick _____   rid _____   piddle _____

fill _____   bid _____   middle _____

3. Change the **e** to **o**:

eat <u>oat</u>   less _____   stew _____

ear _____   let _____   sew _____

bend _____   belt _____   pest _____

4. Change the **o** to **u**:

pot <u>put</u>   cop _____   long _____

dull _____   torn _____   strong _____

role _____   most _____   song _____

Say the old and the new words out loud so you hear the sounds and see the meanings and patterns.

Answers

1 Change **a** to **o**:

cat — <u>cot</u>	paint — <u>point</u>	broad — <u>brood</u>
farmer — <u>former</u>	grain — <u>groin</u>	boat — <u>boot</u>
ward — <u>word</u>	fail — <u>foil</u>	shave — <u>shove</u>
care — <u>core</u>	bath — <u>both</u>	glass — <u>gloss</u>

2. Change the **i** to **e**:

pin — <u>pen</u>	miss — <u>mess</u>	flick — <u>fleck</u>
pick — <u>peck</u>	rid — <u>red</u>	piddle — <u>peddle</u>
fill — <u>fell</u>	bid — <u>bed</u>	middle — <u>meddle</u>

3. Change the **e** to **o**:

eat — <u>oat</u>	less — <u>loss</u>	stew — <u>stow</u>
ear — <u>oar</u>	let — <u>lot</u>	sew — <u>sow</u>
bend — <u>bond</u>	belt — <u>bolt</u>	pest — <u>post</u>

4. Change the **o** to **u**:

pot — <u>put</u>	cop — <u>cup</u>	long — <u>lung</u>
doll — <u>dull</u>	torn — <u>turn</u>	strong — <u>strung</u>
role — <u>rule</u>	most — <u>must</u>	song — <u>sung</u>

Spelling vs. Pronunciation

We're going to look at the differences between spelling and pronunciation in some common words with silent letters in them. We'll see how we can use spelling strategies to successfully spell them. We'll also review memory tricks, syllable breakdown, spelling rules, and phonetic strategies.

In set 1, we're going to look at eight words that are pronounced with two syllables but spelled with three. These are simple words that you might be able to spell now, but read on and go over the spelling strategies.

In Set 2, we'll look at five longer words that are pronounced with three syllables but spelled with four.

These apply to both standard British and American accents.

Exercise Which is correct? Use your spelling strategies to help you. Or you might see what looks right.

1. a. business b. bussiness c. busness

2. a. choclate b. chocolate c. chocalate

3. a. diffrent b. different c. differant

4. a. mariage b. marriage c. marrage

5. a. interesting b. interresting c. intaresting

6. a. Wenesday b. Wednsday c. Wednesday

7. a. temprature b. temperature c. temperuture

8. a. usually b. usualy c. useually

9. a. comfortable b.comfertable c. comfatable

Answers

1. a. business   ~~b. bussiness   c. busness~~

2. ~~a. choclate~~   b. chocolate   ~~c. chocalate~~

3. ~~a. diffrent~~   b. different   ~~c. differant~~

4. ~~a. mariage~~   b. marriage   ~~c. marrage~~

5. a. interesting   ~~b. interresting   c. intaresting~~

6. ~~a. Wenesday   b. Wednsday~~   c. Wednesday

7. ~~a. temprature~~   b. temperature   ~~c. temperuture~~

8. a. usually   ~~b. usualy   c. useually~~

9. a. comfortable   ~~b. comfertable   c. comfatable~~

If you want to listen to the pronunciation (British & American), check these dictionary websites:
www.macmillandictionary.com
www.dictionary.cambridge.org/dictionary/english/
www.merriam-webster.com

Set 1

The following eight words are usually pronounced with two syllables but spelled with three. Breaking these words down into syllables helps if you say them in a slow and exaggerated way, or see words within words, or use memory tricks.

1. business

We say "biz ness" /bɪznɪs/ missing out the 'i' — bus(i)ness
Can you remember the memory trick from the words-within-words section?
*It's good **bus**iness to go by **bus**.*
*Business isn't a **sin**. bus I ness*
Use syllable breakdown: *bus-i-ness*
Remember to add –es for the plural: businesses.

We also have the compound words: *businesswoman*, businesswomen, *businessman, businessmen, businessperson, businesspeople, e-business.*

2. chocolate

We say "choc lat", missing out the 'o' — *choc(o)late.*
Use syllable breakdown: *choc-o-late.*
See the 'o' vowels: chocolate.
*I **ate** too much choco**late**.*

3. different
We say "diff rent", missing out the 'e' — diff(e)rent.
Use syllable breakdown: *dif-fe-rent, dif-fer-ent, diff-e-rent*
*I beg to <u>differ</u> but the **rent** is <u>differ</u>ent every year.*

4. omelette or omelet (BrE) / omelet (AmE)
We say "om let", missing out the 'e' — om(*e)*lette/om(*e)*let
Notice the e's: om**e**lett**e**/om**e**let

Use syllable breakdown:
British: *o-me-lette, om-e-lette*
***Let** me make an omele<u>tte</u> for <u>te</u>a.*

American: *om-e-let*
***Let** me make an ome**let**.*

5. every
We say "ev ry" /evri/, missing out the 'e' — ev(e)ry.
every = e + very
Use syllable breakdown: *ev-e-ry, ev-er-y*
***Every even**ing **Eve** is <u>very</u> tired.*
Also, *everybody, everything, everyone*

6. marriage
We say "ma rige" missing out the 'a' — marri(a)ge.
Spelling rule: *marry + age* change the 'y' to 'i' rule with suffixes.
marry ➜ marri + age = *marriage*
Use syllable breakdown: *mar-ri-age*
*The **age** to marry and have a marr**iage**.*

7. interest
We say "in trest" missing out the 'e' — int(e)rest
Notice the e's: int**e**r**e**st
Use syllable breakdown: *in-te-rest, in-ter-est*
*In the inter**est**s of **inter**national safety, please **rest**.*

8. Wednesday
We say "wens day" /wenz.deɪ/ missing out the 'd' and 'e' — We(d)n(e)sday.
Breaking Wednesday down into syllables is fantastic for remembering the silent **d** and **e**. Remember to say the syllables slowly and exaggeratedly:
Wed-nes-day.

Set 2

The following five words are usually pronounced with three syllables, but spelled with four. Breaking these words down into syllables helps if you say them in a slow and exaggerated way, or see words within words, or use memory tricks.

1. comfortable

We say "comf ta bull" /kʌm fə tə.bᵊl/ missing out the 'or' — comf(or)table.

comfortable = comfort + able

Use syllable breakdown: *com-for-ta-ble, com-fort-able*

2. vegetable

We say "veg t bull" /vedʒ tə bᵊl/ missing out the 'e' — veg(e)table.

Use syllable breakdown: *veg-e-ta-ble,*
Get the veg on the **table** - ve**get**able

3. interesting

We say "in tres ting", missing out the 'e' — int(e)resting.

interesting = interest + ing

Use syllable breakdown: *in-te-rest-ing,   in-ter-est-ing*

Notice the i's and e's: **interesting**

4. temperature

We say "tem pre chu", missing out the 'e' — temp(e)rature.

Use syllable breakdown: *tem-per-a-ture, temp-er-a-ture*

*I get in a **temper** when the **temper**ature is high.*

5. usually

We say "you sh ly", missing out the 'a' — usu(a)lly.

usually = usual + ly (double 'l')

Notice the u's: **u s u** ally

*It's usually **all** or nothing with **us**.*

Even more u's in *unusually* = **un** + **usual** + ly.

186

Exercise

1. a. everybody   b. evrybody   c. evarybody

2. a. unusully   b. unusually   c. unusualy

3. a. Wenesday   b. Wednsday   c. Wednesday

4. a. mariage   b. marriage   c. marryage

5. a. indifferent   b. indifferant   c. indiffrent

6. a. chocolates   b. chocalates   c. choclates

7. a. uncomfortable   b. uncomfortible   c. uncomfotable

8. a. vegtables   b. vegatables   c. vegetables

9. a. interestingly   b. intrestingly   c. intarestingly

10. a. busness   b. bussiness   c. business

Answers

1. a. everybody   b. evrybody   c. evarybody
2. a. unusully   **b. unusually**   c. unusualy
3. a. Wenesday   b. Wednsday   **c. Wednesday**
4. a. mariage   **b. marriage**   c. marryage
5. **a. indifferent**   b. indifferant   c. indiffrent
6. **a. chocolates**   b. chocalates   c. choclates
7. **a. uncomfortable**   b. uncomfortible   c. uncomfotable
8. a. vegtables   b. vegatables   **c. vegetables**
9. a. intrestingly   **b. interestingly**   c. intarestingly
10. a. busness   b. bussiness   **c. business**

Notes

Take an Interest in Words

Taking an interest in words is a key spelling strategy to help you stop getting frustrated with English spelling and start loving it, which, of course, will improve your spelling.

> Enjoy the quirkiness of English spelling, know why words are spelled the way they are, understand the history of spelling, and you won't get frustrated with spelling, and you'll even learn, remember and understand spellings.
> Joanne Rudling: *The Reasons Why English Spelling is so Weird and Wonderful*

> Exploring the origins of words and the processes of word creation provides a powerful knowledge base for learning spelling and vocabulary, as well as facilitating more effective reading and writing.
> Bear, Invernizzi, Templeton, Johnston: *Words Their Way.*

Remember from the Silent Letters section that English and spelling developed from the tribes that invaded and settled in England. Look at the origins of these words below:

> ➤ The **Romans** from Italy (Latin) — *plumber, scissors, debt, receipt...*
> ➤ The **Angles**, **Saxons**, and **Jutes** from Germany and Holland (Dutch/Germanic) — *right, daughter, folk, write, walk...*
> ➤ The **Vikings** from Denmark and Norway (spoke Old Norse) — *know, knee, gnat, gnaw...*
> ➤ And finally, the **French** from northern France (Norman French) changed a lot of spellings. Can you remember why we have *hour, honest, guess, vogue...?*

There's never been a moment when English was pure. English has always been influenced by other languages, and has never been afraid of borrowing words from everywhere.

We've never had an academy of English to control our words, spelling, or language, which is why we have a huge variety of words, "strange" spellings, and an enormous dictionary and thesaurus.

➜ Where do you think these words come from?
1. bungalow	2. ketchup	3. galore
4. alcohol	5. guru	6. shampoo

Answers on page 191

> Most of the borrowings in Modern English have been in the language for centuries, as a result of the first periods of contact, so we no longer have a sense of their foreign-ness.
>
> David Crystal: *Words Words Words*

In the 17th-19th centuries, the British Empire expanded and introduced words from all parts of the world, and with them some strange spellings:

America — *prairie*

India — *chutney*

Australia — *kangaroo*

New Zealand — *kiwi*

Africa — *safari*

China — *ketchup*

Words and spellings can even show us the trade undertaken and history of exploration. It also gives us a sense of the country:

- India: *guru, bungalow, veranda, juggernaut, pundit, shampoo, chintz*
- Words from Holland and the Dutch include words about art: *easel, etch, landscape*. From seafaring: *smuggle, cruise*
- Travels to South America borrowed from Spanish and Portuguese include *tobacco, hurricane, banana, alligator, potato*
- Italian: *violin, solo, sonnet, giraffe, balcony*

We have food products from all over the world:
- French: *almond, salad, lettuce, basil, spinach, rice, mustard*
- Spanish: *avocado, potato*
- Portuguese: *coconut*
- Italian: *pasta, pesto, broccoli*
- Tamil: *curry*
- Dutch: *cookie*
- Chinese: *pak choi/bok choi, ketchup*
- Latin: *wine, cheese, peas*
- Arabic: *coffee, alcohol, sugar, syrup*

Answers

1. **bungalow** from India, Hindi *bangla* 'belonging to Bengal', from a type of cottage built for early European settlers in Bengal.

2. **ketchup** from Chinese Cantonese dialect, tomato juice.

3. **galore** (not mentioned above, but can you guess?) from Irish *go leor*, literally 'to sufficiency'.

4. **alcohol** from Arabic *al-kuhl* 'the kohl'. In early use, the term referred to powders, specifically kohl, and especially those obtained by distilling or rectifying spirits.

5. **guru** from India, Hindi and Punjabi, from Sanskrit *guru* 'one to be honoured/honored, teacher, venerable'.

6. **shampoo** from India, Hindi *campo!* "press!"

Next, we're going to look at British and American spelling next.

➔Which are the American spellings and why are there differences?

car tyre or tire
colour or color
fulfil or fulfill
travelling or traveling
enrol or enroll
realise or realize
centre or center

American vs. British Spelling

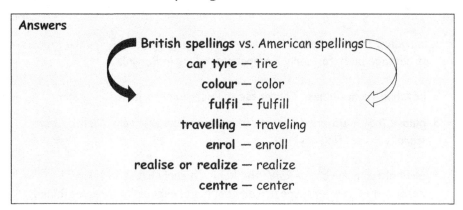
Knowing the differences between American and British English spelling is important because of the internet and computer software. Also, a lot of computers are automatically set to an American dictionary, so if you're working in British English, it will leave you wondering why your spelling has a red squiggly line under it, even though you spelt it correctly!

When you know the differences, you can adapt your spelling to whatever person or market you're writing for.

Knowing the differences adds another layer to your spelling knowledge and stops potential confusion.

➜ So why are there differences?

During the American Revolution (1775-1783), the Americans overthrew British rule and wanted to be different from Britain — and one way was to reform spelling. Noah Webster led the way.

In 1783, he published a book called the *American Spelling Book*, which sold millions, and in 1828, he published his *American English Dictionary*.

Noah Webster (1758-1843)
Born Hartford, Connecticut, United States

The main spelling reforms were reducing the number of letters and changing some letters around.

British to **American**
-our to -**or**
(colour to **color**)

-re to -**er**
(centre to **center**)

-ise to -**ize**
(realise to **realize**)

-yse to -**yze**
(analyse to **analyze**)

-ogue to -**og** or -**ogue**
(dialogue to **dialogue** or **dialog**)

British to *American*
-**our** to -*or*
colour — *color*
honour — *honor*
flavour — *flavor*
humour — *humor*
labour — *labor*
odour — *odor*
rumour — *rumor*
saviour — *savior*
favourite — *favorite*
behaviour — *behavior*
neighbour — *neighbor*
harbour — *harbor*
savoury — *savory*
splendour — *splendor*
demeanour — *demeanor*
glamour — *glamour*
less commonly *glamor*

Be careful,
American spelling
still has:
our, your, hour,
four, flour, dour,
sour, tour, scour,
detour, devour,
contour, pour,
velour

British to *American*

-re to *-er*

centre — *center*

metre — *meter*

fibre — *fiber*

litre — *liter*

sombre — *somber*

centimetre — *centimeter*

theatre — *theater* or *theatre*

These words are still spelled with **-re** in American: *acre, massacre, lucre, mediocre, ogre.*

-ise to **-ize**

According to the *Oxford Dictionary*, both endings are correct in British English but only one way in American. Canadians usually use **-ize**. They recommend you choose one style and stick to it within a piece of writing. The *Oxford Dictionary* uses the **-ize** ending on their website, probably because the **-ize** ending is older and closer to its Greek roots. But **-ise** is more widely used.

British English -ise or ize	American English -ize
realise or realize	realize
apologise or apologize	apologize
organise or organize	organize
recognise or recognize	recognise or recognize
finalise or finalize	finalize

CAREFUL, a few words must only be spelled with **-ise**:

advertise, advise, chastise, compromise, despise, devise, disguise, excise, exercise, improvise, promise.

No doubling of the final 'l'
This applies to words of more than one syllable ending in 'l' when adding a vowel suffix/ending.

British: cancel — cancelling, cancelled, cancellation
American: cancel — canceling, canceled, cancelation

British: marvel — marvellous, marvelled, marvelling
American: marvel — marvelous, marveled, marveling

British: travel — travelling, travelled, traveller
American: travel — traveling, traveled, traveler

British: jewel — jewellery, jeweller
American: jewel — jewelry, jeweler

British — *American*
modelled/modelling — *modeled/modeling*
quarelled/quarelling — *quarreled/quarreling*
counsellor — *counselor*
equalled — *equaled*
fuelling/fuelled — *fueling/fueled*
grovelled/grovelling — *groveled/groveling*
woollen — *woolen*

This also applies to a few American words when the stress falls on a syllable other than the first.

conTROL   paTROL
controlled   *patrolled*
controlling   *patrolling*
annulled, expelled, extolled

Be careful with these words:
British English: enrol - *enrolling, enrolled*
American English: *enroll* ends in double 'l', so *enrolling, enrolled.*

Both American and British agree not to double the end 'l' in parallel —
parallels, paralleling, paralleled.

But be careful with these words:

British single "l" — American double "l"

appal — appall

distil — distill

enrol — enroll

enthral — enthrall

fulfil — fulfill

instil — instill

skilful — skillful

wilful — willful

Let's look at some more spelling differences between American and British words. In most cases, American words have fewer letters.

American — **British**

licorice — liquorice

program — programme but computer program

maneuve — manoeuvre

sulfur — sulphur

naught — nought

skeptic — sceptic

vial — phial

→ Do you know the British spellings of these American spellings?

write a *check* —

cozy —

donut —

roadside curb —

mustache —

omelet —

pajamas —

car tire —

gray —

math —

Answers

Am — write a check
Br — cheque

Am — cozy
Br — cosy

Am — donut
Br — doughnut

Am — roadside curb
Br — kerb

Am — mustache
Br — moustache

Am — omelet
Br — omelette

Am — pajamas
Br — pyjamas

Am — tire
Br — tyre

Am — gray
Br — grey

Am — math
Br — maths

American or British?

The following words are useful to know so we can understand each other on holiday/vacation, in restaurants, watching films and TV shows, etc.

Clothes

American	British
pants	trousers
underwear / panties	pants / knickers / underwear
sneakers	trainers
diaper	nappy
sweater	jumper / sweater / pullover
turtle neck	polo neck

Food

American	British
zucchini	courgette
eggplant	aubergine
cookie	biscuit
candy	sweets
jelly	jam
jello	jelly
potato chips	crisps
fries/ French fries	chips
arugula	rocket
cilantro	coriander
takeout	takeaway
check	bill
napkin	serviette

American	British
flashlight	torch
Band-Aid	plaster
fall	autumn
national holiday	bank holiday
elevator	lift
stand in line	queue
There's a line	There's a queue
ladybug	ladybird
trash can	dustbin/rubbish bin/bin
closet	wardrobe
sidewalk	pavement
parking lot	car park
gas/gasoline	petrol
fire truck	fire engine
freeway	motorway
vacation	holiday

Job Application Words

+ revision of some words

We all know how important it is to spell perfectly on application forms, and on your CV (curriculum vitae) (BrE) / résumé (AmE).

If you don't know, or are unsure of a spelling, then use a dictionary or online dictionary. When we don't use certain words all the time, we tend to forget how to spell them, so please, please, please use a dictionary.

Self-Assessment Exercise

Do you know how to spell the important words below?
Can you use any spelling strategies to help?

1. a. referrence b. reference c. referance

2. a. sucessful b. succesfull c. successful

3. a. beginner b. beginer c. begginner

4. a. tommorrow b. tomorrow c. tommorow

5. a. achievable b. achieveable c. acheivable

6. a. responsibilitys b. responsibilties c. responsibilities

7. a. preference b. preferrence c. prefference

8. a. particulary b. particulalary c. particularly

9. a. communacator b. communicator c. comunnicator

10. a. experiance b. experience c. experrience

11. a. applying b. appliing c. aplying

12. a. applycation b. aplication c. application

13. a. forward b. foreward c. forrward

14. a. coleague b. colleague c. collegue

Answers

1. a. referrence   **b. reference**   c. referance
2. a. sucessful   b. succesfull   **c. successful**
3. **a. beginner**   b. beginer   c. begginner
4. a. tommorrow   **b. tomorrow**   c. tommorow
5. **a. achievable**   b. achieveable   c. acheivable
6. a. responsibilitys   b. responsibilties   **c. responsibilities**
7. **a. preference**   b. preferrence   c. prefference
8. a. particulary   b. particulolary   **c. particularly**
9. a. communacator   **b. communicator**   c. comunnicator
10. a. experiance   **b. experience**   c. expernience
11. **a. applied**   b. applyed   c. aplied
12. a. applycation   b. aplication   **c. application**
13. **a. forward**   b. foreward   c. forrward
14. a. coleague   **b. colleague**   c. collegue

My responsibilities included liaising with managers and communicating with customer services.

Applicants should demonstrate a familiarity with housing regulations.

I would like to apply for the position of Environmental Liaison Officer.

I have five years' experience as an office manager.

The single word most commonly misspelled is **"responsibility"**, a worrying error considering how many people use it to flag up their attractions to potential employers. (*telegraph.co.uk*)

responsibility — responsibility (notice all the i's)
responsibility = *responsible* - drop the 'le' and add –ility

Break it into syllables: re/spon/sib/il/i/ty or re/spon/si/bil/ity

(plural) **responsibilities** — the end 'y' becomes 'ies'
(notice all the i's: responsibilities)

Responsibility sounds like and has the same –**ility** pattern as these words. (This naturally breaks into syllables so helps with the spelling.)
ability, agility, civility, docility, utility, futility, facility, fertility, stability, liability, hostility, versatility, mobility, tranquility, humility, fragility...

---

apply
applying
Remember to change the 'y' to 'i' with suffixes except –ing and -ish
applied
application ("ap-pli-ca-tion" — syllable breakdown)
applicable ("ap-pli-ca-ble")
applicant ("ap-pli-cant")

Remember the "**ha**ppy" words.
I was happy to apply and I filled in an application with all the applicable information.

---

success (double 'c' and double 's')
Double Congratulations on your Super Success.
Constant Congratulations on your Super Success.
successful = success + ful = *successful / unsuccessful*
successfully = success + ful + ly = *successfully / unsuccessfully*
unsuccessful = un + success + ful = *unsuccessful*
unsuccessfully = un + success + ful + ly = *unsuccessfully*

succeed (double 'c' and double 'e')
Only 3 words end in –**ceed**: *exceed, succeed, proceed.*

I succeeded in exceeding their expectations and will now proceed exceedingly quickly and successfully.

achieve ("i before e except after c" rule applies)
achieved
achieving (drop the 'e' with –ing)
achievable (drop the 'e' with –able)
achievement, achievements (keep the 'e')
It gave me a great sense of achievement to achieve top marks in the test.

→Think of some memory tricks and sentences for the following words.

refer
double 'r' — **referring, referred, referral, referrer** (doubling up rule)
single 'r' — **reference, referee, referendum** (Notice all the e's.)

liaise Notice those i's.
liaison (drop the 'e' and add -on)
Use the first letters to make up a saying: *Live in an igloo, son*
liaising (drop the 'e' + ing)

communicate We communicate through **Mass Media.**
communicator
communication

experience Notice all the e's and **i** in the middle "ex pe ri ence".
experienced
inexperience/inexperienced

manage
managing (drop the 'e' with –ing)
managed
manager
management (manage + ment)
manageable (keep the 'e' to keep the 'g' soft)

environment (don't forget the "iron")
environment — environmental — environmentally

committee — Many Meetings are Terribly Tedious.
commit **to** the commi**tt**ee is especially **e**asy

---

colleague ("col-league")
colleagues

---

collaboration
collaborate — collaborating — collaboration — collaborator — collaborative

---

questionnaire (double n) question + naire

Questionnaire and *legionnaire* are borrowed from French.

Be careful, **single n** in *billionaire, extraordinaire, millionaire,
Apollinaire, commissionaire, concessionaire...*

---

entrepreneur Can you see all those e's? entr**e**pr**e**n**e**ur
entre pre neur

---

particular (syllable breakdown "par tic u lar")
particular + ly = **particularly**

---

begin
beginning (1:1:1 doubling up rule)
beginnings
beginner

---

familiar I'm *familiar* with that *peculiar* liar.
familiarise / familiarize
familiarity ("fa-mil-i-a-ri-ty")

---

tomorrow "Good morrow" was the old way of saying good day.
to + morrow = tomorrow

tomorrow/borrow/sorrow/furrow/marrow/arrow/sparrow

Letter endings

⇨**I look forward to hearing from you.**
hearing (ear), hear, hearing, heard

for + ward = *forward*
straightforward, henceforward

-ward(s) = direction: *forward (towards the future), towards, onward, upward, backward, sideward, homeward, eastward, westward...*

⇨**Yours sincerely,**
(use when you know their name: Dear Jane Smith, Dear Miss Smith.)
since + rely = sincerely (***since I sincerely rely** on you*)
(Also in AmE — Sincerely yours)

Yours sincerely, Joanne
Sincerely yours, Joanne

⇨**Yours faithfully**
(Use *faithfully* when you don't know the name and using Dear Sir/Madam.)
faith + ful + l y = faithfully

Now write a personal statement about your experience, job responsibilities, goals and achievements.

Or just write some sentences with these job application words.

Revision Exercise

Which are correct? Use your strategies to help.
If you're not sure, then go back and check.

1. a. unneccesary b. unnecessary c. unecessary

2. a. embarrasing b. embarrassing c. embarassing

3. a. tomorow b. tommorrow c. tomorrow

4. a. signifecant b. significent c. significant

5. a. Wednsday b. Wenesday c. Wednesday

6. 40 = a. fourty b. fourrty c. forty

7. 9th = a. nineth b. ninth c. nineneth

8. a. business b. bussiness c. businness

9. a. occasionally b. ocasionally c. occasionaly

10. a. questionaire b. questionnaire c. questionnare

11. a. referrence b. referance c. reference

12. a. experience b. experiance c. expearience

13. a. truely b. truly c. truley

14. a. responsibilities b. responsabilities c. responsibilties

15. a. acheivements b. achievments c. achievements

16. a. sincerley b. sincerely c. sincearly

Answers

1. a. unneccesary   b. **unnecessary**   c. unecessary

2. a. embarrasing   b. **embarrassing**   c. embarassing

3. a. tomorow   b. tommorrow   c. **tomorrow**

4. a. signifecant   b. significent   c. **significant**

5. a. Wednsday   b. Wenesday   c. **Wednesday**

6. 40 = a. fourty   b. fourrty   c. **forty**

7. 9th = a. nineth   b. **ninth**   c. nineneth

8. a. **business**   b. bussiness   c. businness

9. a. **occasionally**   b. ocasionally   c. occasionaly

10. a. questionaire   b. **questionnaire**   c. questionnare

11. a. referrence   b. referance   c. **reference**

12. a. **experience**   b. experiance   c. expearience

13. a. truely   b. **truly**   c. truley

14. a. **responsibilities**   b. responsabilities   c. responsibilties

15. a. acheivements   b. achievments   c. **achievements**

16. a. sincerley   b. **sincerely**   c. sincearly

Your Spelling Stories

You're not alone in wanting help with spelling. I get emails every day from native speakers in the UK, USA, Australia, Canada, and more who feel let down by their education. These people are in their 30s to 60s. I even get students in college and high school who struggle with their spelling and need help.

Now more than ever, we need to spell and write with confidence. We rely on emails and social media to stay in touch with our friends and colleagues, to feel part of society, and to belong to our social groups. This need, or pressure, to be social involves writing, but it might be that more people are engaging by sharing videos and cute pictures rather than writing how they feel because they don't want to embarrass themselves with their spelling.

I can see how some people struggle with spelling when they write comments or Facebook updates, and it's painful to see. I don't judge these people, but others will. Part of the problem is people don't proofread their words. Another problem is predictive text; I don't know how many times I've made a mistake by typing too quickly and missed or transposed a letter, only to find the predictive text has written something completely different than I intended. No matter what, always, always proofread the tiniest email, comment, etc.

In this section are some of the emails I've received from around the world. When necessary, I've proofread and corrected typos and punctuation to make it easier to read, but the stories are all in their own words.

> I'm 57, a grandma, and work online. I lost jobs over my spelling and was so depressed. Spelling has always held me back in life but not anymore. I feel differently about spelling now because I understand it better. Alison, UK

> I work in my local hospital on a maternity unit - we're called maternity support workers. We need to write in the mother's notes but I've always shied away from writing in them because of my spelling and my handwriting - it's so embarrassing. Anyway, since doing your course, I've noticed my handwriting and spelling have improved. I can't explain how much this means to me and to say thank you. The confidence I have, I feel like I'm walking on air. And if you would have told me I would be writing this email this time last week, I would have said no way. Annette, UK

> Thank you so much for all your lessons. I have been trying to spell, it's not easy. I'm 52 and do lots of things helping others but when it comes to writing names and address, I just seize up. Pauline, Ireland

I was brought up in the fifties and I am naturally left-handed, but was made to write with my right hand as left-handers are backward! So from the age of five to ten, I refused to write. That changed when I was hit (on my right hand) by Sister Angela with the edge of the ruler in front of the whole class and told to return to my desk and write! Which I did, but this time, I could only use my left hand and was left alone to do so!!! However, that experience has not left me, or being tagged as backward!!! E. G. USA

I've improved so much in my spelling, and I'm less embarrassed and afraid to write on paper or on the computer than I was before I started these lessons. It's a worthwhile journey for me.

When I was in primary school, I tried using vocabulary in my composition in class and, as you can imagine, I got all the spellings wrong for all the vocabulary I tried to use. My teacher read the composition and embarrassed me so much that I vowed never to learn anymore vocabulary, well, until I came across your website and learned all the tricks. Now I can use and learn new words and spell the tricky ones. Sherry, UK.

My experience at school was awful, the worst time of my life. Nothing made any sense to me, the letters just kept moving around on the paper. The headmaster told my parents that I was mentally abnormal, said they couldn't teach me anything. I left school unable to read or write.

At 15, I went straight into factory work. I managed to work for 24 years. I taught myself to read and write a little but my spelling is not very good. Thanks to you I'm getting better and more confident. David.

The biggest reason that I didn't go to school in the first and second grades was because of "Spelling Bees". I was just too embarrassed to attend class, so I just told everyone that I was sick so they would keep me home. Although I'm sure that Spelling Bees are a very useful tool for teachers, I was never so embarrassed in my life.

To this day, I feel very sorry for children that are now going through what I had to when I was young. Can you imagine trying to say something with everyone staring at just you and not knowing what to say? I hated school because of Spelling Bees, along with having to get up in front of the class: too much of being put on display, in my book. HK, USA

I don't know how I found you on the internet, but am so pleased I did. I was looking for a basic English course at my local college (well, spelling really), just a refresher course. You have saved me the embarrassment of attending college by sending me great work I can do at home. I love doing the spelling tests, etc. and with so much to choose from, I feel I have improved in such a short time. The spelling patterns, rules, words-within-words - why did I never see that? I am so grateful to you for your help. Regards, Christine, UK

I am 57 years old and just watched the first video session with "able". Wish I had you as my English teacher back in my primary years. This is the first time I actually enjoyed learning to spell. Your method of teaching will also help my little 6-year-old grandson to learn to spell. Thank you. Jill, UK

I'm 44 years old and I've always had a problem with spelling. I work in an organization where I need to communicate in English. Sometimes, I have to stand up in meetings and write on a whiteboard. You can imagine how difficult it is if you have bad spelling. However, now I use spelling strategies to help and I feel much better. Y, Qatar

I'm sixty years old and never really liked spelling when I was at school. I started a website a few years ago, which helped me somewhat with my spelling, but I no longer have it.

I work for a big supermarket and have just started on security so need to be able to spell. I think I tend to spell words the way they sound. So I think it's a matter of going through and trying to memorise/memorize the spelling patterns and use memory tricks. Trev, UK

I'm doing my GCSE maths and English level 2 — that will help me get into my career. Hope to meet you in the future. You're much better than MPs and people that are in charge of education.

In my opinion, I think many people run away from school because they don't teach something that makes sense. People won't spend hours practising (practicing — AmE) something but your course is easy to understand and straightforward. Adan, London

I just want to be good at English so I can do more things. I have an idea for writing books but am unable to write it down because of my problems with spelling and grammar. After listening to your voice on your videos, I was surprised how happy I was. Chris, UK

My spelling demons have been haunting me for years, but even more recently because I have to teach and create presentations at a professional level. In my case, I lost out on the early years of school because of eye troubles and never really got to catch up. Whilst not officially tested, I am convinced that I suffer with dyslexia. You can imagine the embarrassment and frustration I try to hide on a daily basis. Anyway, I am sure that my story is not dissimilar to so many others and now at 41 years old, I am finally getting the help and support I need.

Now that I understand that there is a logic to spelling, it excites me to learn patterns and word sums, etc. and the memory tricks are great too - here's one of mine! "It's only *visible* with two eyes (i's)."

Even after a few days of using the strategies, my spelling has measurably improved and I am starting to enjoy writing for the first time in my life. Credit where credit is due. Matt, Ireland

It has been a while but since we last talked I have published two papers and been massively involved in a university-related project. So my time is at a premium these days. I would like to tell you that my spelling really has improved but more importantly is my confidence. Often now I question words that I never would have before. When this happens, I visit the online Oxford Dictionary which has become like a friend. Matt, Ireland

My Spelling Experience by Darren Johnson, UK

School should be the best times of our lives, that's what people say, so why did so many of us get let down by school?

I started infant school in the early 70s and finished secondary school in 1982, and it still hurts me to this day how let down I feel with my schooling, and teachers who were happy with their day's work by not bothering. My history teacher used to say, "if you don't want to learn, I'll sign you in and you can go home until the next class".

It's the most precious time in our lives because it sets us up for the rest of our lives, and yes, it set a lot of us up on the scrap heap!

I was allowed to leave school at fourteen because my mum and dad split up and I moved away with my mum and two brothers. So I missed the last two years and didn't take any exams - how could they have allowed this?

I can remember being in remedial English with only six of us there. When asked to read a book, I would say I can't because the words were moving - was this fear or just trying to hide, or dyslexia?
I feel so hurt by my schooling. Or did this set me up in life to work with my hands, which I've been lucky enough to do?

Enough of me moaning. 25 years after leaving school, I felt I owed it to myself to stop hiding from spelling and try and do something about it. I've been working really hard the last eight years to try and improve. I feel I've come a long way but I know I have at least another five years to get to where I want to be.

It's amazing - in the last eight years I've taken my Level 1 and 2 English and Maths exams and passed. This is something you should pass when you're 16 years old - I feel a fool but also very proud.

So now I'm 50 this year and I want to get more into management but need to spell a lot better. Lucky for me, we all have spell- check on our phones and computers. But my spelling was so bad that my computer couldn't even help me.

After trying so many different ways to spell, I've learnt the only way that works for me is writing a word down twenty times a day for two weeks. After a few months, you start to see you only need to add a few letters and you have a new word. So you start to learn that you don't need to learn a 8 or 9 letter word - you just need to add a few letters to the 4 or 6 letter word you've learnt.

I now find it really easy to spell *friend* but after reading a few books, I see that lots of people find this hard. I just look at the "*end*" on the end and 'i' before 'e' so all I need to know is "fr". I could never spell *Chris* but all I do is think "is" on the end and then all I need now is "Chr".

For years, when spelling a person's name like *Brian,* I would put Brain, but little tips like just put *Ian* on the end just like *Julian.*

I was never taught how to break words down as a kid, let alone spelling strategies, rules, prefixes and suffixes. Now I'm reading shop fronts, and vans with writing on and noticing lots of words with words in them. It's amazing how it's slowly coming together.

The happy ending! I'm a director of a construction company. We work for a lot of VIPs. We're very lucky with work. We're always turning it away. So as you can see I've done very well. I'm a Chartered Builder or a Chartered Construction Manager. I have a level 7 in Site Management plus level 6 and 3, and many more different NVQs. So I have letters after my name when I need to use them for work!

References and Further Reading

Murray Suid: *Demonic Mnemonics* (Fearon)
Shireen Shuster: *Spelling Essentials* (Longman)
Joy Pollock: *Signposts to Spelling* (Blessings)
Gena K. Gorrell: *"Say What?" (Tundra Books)*
David Crystal: *Words Words Words* (Oxford)
David Crystal: *The Stories of English* (Penguin)
David Crystal: *The English Language* (
Larry Beason: *Eyes before Ease* (McGraw-Hill)
Anne Betteridge: *Adult Learners' Guide to Spelling* (Chambers)
Catherine Taylor: *A Useful Spelling Handbook for Adults* (Olympia)
G. Terry Page: *The Book of Spelling Rules* (Wordsworth Reference)
Meryl Wilkins: *Improve our Spelling in English* (NIACE)
Pacquita Boston: *The Inside Story of Spelling*

For Teachers

Spelling Pack (Basic Skills Agency)
The Starter Pack (1st edition) (Basic Skills Agency)
Johanna Stirling: *Teaching Spelling to English Language Learners*
Sally Raymond: *Spelling Rules, Riddles and Remedies* (Routledge)
Bear, Invernizzi, Templeton, Johnston: *Words Their Way* (Pearson)
Lyn Stone: *Spelling For Life* (Routledge)
Edward Carney: *English Spelling* (Routledge)
Sue Abell: *Helping Adults to Spell* (ALBSU)
Cynthia. Klein: *Learning to Spell — or Spelling to Learn* (ALBSU)
Cynthia Klein: *Unscrambling Spelling*
D.W. Cummings: *American English Spelling* (John Hopkins)
David Crystal: *Spell it Out* (Profile Books)
Research Paper: Kelly, Soundranayagam, Grief: *Teaching and learning writing: a review of research and practice.* June 2004. (National Research and Development Centre for adult literacy and numeracy.)

Websites

www.howtospell.co.uk   www.bbc.co.uk/skillswise
www.beatingdyslexia.com   www.grammar-monster.com

Online Dictionaries with pronunciation and example sentences

www.oxforddictionaries.com — British & American
www.macmillandictionary.com — British & American
https://dictionary.cambridge.org — British & American
www.merriam-webster.com — American

About the Author

Joanne Rudling is a freelance lecturer, teacher trainer, and owner of www.howtospell.co.uk.

She's taught spelling, literacy and writing for 20 years in various organizations including: City of Westminster College, Bournemouth FE College, Dorset Adult Education, Bournemouth University, and Bournemouth Film School.

Joanne has developed and taught on literacy projects for the Pre-Volunteer Programme for the Olympics, and the RNIB (Royal National Institute for the Blind).

She's also edited closed captions/subtitles from American spellings to British for Amazon.com TV drama division.

Other books by Joanne on Amazon, & howtospell.co.uk
Spelling Rules Workbook — a step-by-step guide to the rules of English spelling (hard copy and ebook)
How to Spell the 20 Most Commonly Misspelled Words (hard copy)
QTS Spelling Strategies to Help You Pass the Literacy Skills Spelling Test (hard copy and ebook)
Punctuation Guide and Workbook (hard copy and ebook)
The Reasons Why English Spelling is so Weird and Wonderful (ebook)

For kids
Spelling Rules and Patterns for Ages 10-11: To learn, improve & have fun with spelling and writing (For British English)
Spelling Patterns and Rules for 5th Graders: To learn, improve & have fun with spelling (For American English)

Online video courses on udemy.com
Spelling Rules: to improve spelling & confidence (A step-by-step how to spell guide for British & American English)

How to Punctuate Spelling: to improve spelling & writing (From apostrophes to hyphens - an intermediate course to understand and master the tricky punctuation marks in spellings)

Online video courses on curious.com/howtospell
Rules of English Spelling
Beginner's Guide to English Punctuation
ESL Spelling Strategies

Last Page Quickie Quiz — 16 Common Misspellings

Multiple choice exercises can really mess with your brain because they present you with spelling alternatives which also look right! So, use spelling strategies to help you.

Check your answers below. For the memory tricks or rules check the pages listed here.

1. Which one is a sweet, pudding, etc.
   a. desert (page — 75)
   b. dessert

2. a. cemetery (page — 54, 123)
   b. cematery
   c. cemetary

3. a. aparrent (page — 33, 49)
   b. apparent
   c. apparrent

4. a. equipmet (page — 154)
   b. equipment
   c. equiptment

5. a. definately (page — 34, 151)
   b. definetely
   c. definitely

6. a. maintenance (page — 179)
   b. maintenence
   c. maintainance

7. a. grateful (page — 146, 178)
   b. gratefull
   c. greatful

8. a. embarassment (page — 45)
   b. embarrasment
   c. embarrassment

9. a. harass (page — 45)
   b. harrass

10. a. calender (page — 34)
    b. calendar

11. a. believe (page — 31)
    b. beleive

12. a. disappear (page — 49)
    b. dissappear
    c. disapear

13. a. necesary (page — 44)
    b. necessary
    c. neccessary

14. a. niece (page — 55)
    b. neice

15. a. completly (page — 48, 151)
    b. completely

16. a. recommend (page — 48)
    b. reccommend
    c. reccomend

➔If you've made a mistake, think about it and see if you can use a strategy to help you.

➔Keep writing the words you want to spell; use Look, Say, Cover, Write; also record them as a spelling test and test yourself again and again.

(Answers: 1.b 2.a 3.b 4.b 5.c 6.a 7.a 8.c 9.a 10.b 11.a 12.a 13.b 14.a 15.b 16 a)

Made in the USA
Las Vegas, NV
05 April 2024

88272354R00118